| 中国思想文化术语多语种对外翻译
标准化建设项目成果
CHINESE THINKING AND CULTURE
MULTILINGUAL TERMINOLOGY DATABASE

中华源·河南故事
CHINESE CIVILIZATION
Stories from Henan

TAIJIQUAN

主编　王建修
EDITOR-IN-CHIEF: WANG JIANXIU

河南大学出版社
HENAN UNIVERSITY PRESS
·郑州·

## 图书在版编目（CIP）数据

中华源·河南故事. 太极拳 / 王建修主编. -- 郑州：河南大学出版社，2019.3（2021.12重印）

ISBN 978-7-5649-2563-5

Ⅰ. ①中… Ⅱ. ①王… Ⅲ. ①地方文化－河南－通俗读物②太极拳－通俗读物 Ⅳ. ① G127.61-49 ② G852.11-49

中国版本图书馆CIP数据核字（2019）第 047033 号

| | |
|---|---|
| 责任编辑 | 陈林涛 |
| 责任校对 | 韩　琳　屈琳玉 |
| 封面设计 | 翟淼淼 |
| 出版发行 | 河南大学出版社 |
| | 地址：郑州市郑东新区商务外环中华大厦2401号　邮编：450046 |
| | 电话：0371-86059701（营销部）　0371-86059753（大众读物分公司） |
| | 网址：hupress.henu.edu.cn |
| 排　　版 | 河南大学出版社设计排版部 |
| 印　　刷 | 河南博雅彩印有限公司 |
| 版　　次 | 2020年5月第1版　　　　　　　　印　次　2021年12月第2次印刷 |
| 开　　本 | 710 mm×1010 mm　1/16　　　　印　张　12 |
| 字　　数 | 167千　　　　　　　　　　　　　定　价　72.00元 |

版权所有，侵权必究

本书如有印装质量问题，请与河南大学出版社营销部联系调换。

## "中华源·河南故事"系列丛书编委会

顾　　问　　黄友义　杨　平　范大祺
名誉主任　　穆为民　何金平
主　　任　　付　静
副 主 任　　陈志伟　刁玉华　李向前　李　镇　梁留科
　　　　　　刘金锋　孔留安　史永庆　许二平　万正峰
　　　　　　杨建伟　杨玮斌　王建修　王自文　张改平
　　　　　　张松文　赵卫东

主　　编　　付　静
执行主编　　杨玮斌
编　　委　　陈　玮　丁　锐　高　阳　徐恒振

## 中华源·河南故事·太极拳

主　　编　　王建修
副 主 编　　严双军　毛燕翔　赵　昉（英文）
中文撰稿　　严双军
英文译者　　冉玉体　朱宝锋　蔺志渊　秦　琴　赵　昉
英文审校　　〔美〕Thomas K. Alexander
摄　　影　　周双林

# The Editorial Committee
## *Chinese Civilization*
## *Stories from Henan*

| | |
|---|---|
| Consultants | Huang Youyi   Yang Ping   Fan Daqi |
| Honorary Directors | Mu Weimin   He Jinping |
| Director | Fu Jing |
| Deputy Directors | Chen Zhiwei   Diao Yuhua   Li Xiangqian   Li Zhen |
| | Liang Liuke   Liu Jinfeng   Kong Liu'an   Shi Yongqing |
| | Xu Erping   Wan Zhengfeng   Yang Jianwei |
| | Yang Weibin   Wang Jianxiu   Wang Ziwen |
| | Zhang Gaiping   Zhang Songwen |
| | Zhao Weidong |

| | |
|---|---|
| Chief Editor | Fu Jing |
| Executive Chief Editor | Yang Weibin |
| Editors | Chen Wei   Ding Rui   Gao Yang   Xu Hengzhen |

## *Chinese Civilization*
## *Stories from Henan*
### *Taijiquan*

| | |
|---|---|
| Editor-in-Chief | Wang Jianxiu |
| Associate Editors-in-Chief | Yan Shuangjun   Mao Yanxiang |
| | Zhao Fang (English Text) |
| Writer | Yan Shuangjun |
| Translators | Ran Yuti   Zhu Baofeng   Lin Zhiyuan   Qin Qin |
| | Zhao Fang |
| Translation Proofreader | Thomas K. Alexander (USA) |
| Photographer | Zhou Shuanglin |

# 总 序

中国是世界四大文明古国之一，也是世界上唯一的古代文明传统未曾中断的国家。河南省地处中国中东部，是中华文明和中华民族的重要发祥地，在中国五千年的文明史上，河南作为国家政治、经济、文化的中心就长达三千多年。从某种意义上讲，一部河南史就是半部中国史。这里是中华人文始祖黄帝的故乡，是古丝绸之路的东方起点，是少林功夫和陈氏太极的发源地，这里创建了中国历史上最早的都城，镌刻了中国最古老的文字，诞生了中国最初的商业文明。

伴随着新时代的荣光，河南经济社会发展迅速，人民生活水平显著提升，这是自力更生、艰苦奋斗的历史结果，也是对外开放带来的益处。河南经济社会的发展、人民生活方式的改变都植根于深层次的文化积淀。为了让世界更多地了解河南，让河南更好地走向世界，2018年以来，河南省外事办认真研析了这片古老土地上的历史文化资源和时代风貌，组织各领域权威专家学者，编译了"中华源·河南故事"中外文系列丛书，选取少林功夫、太极拳、中医、汉字、文物、焦裕禄、红旗渠、丝绸之路、古都、手工艺、农业等多个主题，力图以故事的方式向世界展现一个立体、全面、真实的河南。

当今世界，人类文明无论在物质还是精神方面都取得了巨大进步，特别是物质的极大丰富是古代世界完全不能想象的。同时，当代人类也面临着许多突出的难题，比如，贫富差距持续扩大，物欲追求奢华无度，个人主义恶性膨胀，社会诚信不断消减，伦理道德每况愈下，人与自然关系日趋紧张，等等。要解决这些难题，不仅需要运用人类今天发现和发展的智慧和力量，而且需要运用人类历史上积累和储存的智慧和力量。河南历史文化底蕴深厚、包容性强，在今天仍极具现实意义。中原文化蕴含的思想智慧有助于修身养性，推动人类社会进步发展，焦裕禄精神、红旗渠精神所体现的为民爱民、艰苦奋斗的价值取向是构建人类命运共同体的力量源泉。我们期待与读者们一起从河南故事中汲取更多的智慧和力量，共同创造更加美好的未来。

# Series Foreword

China is one of the four ancient civilizations in the world, and is also the only country in the world where the ancient civilization has not been interrupted. Located in east-central China, Henan province is an important cradle for the Chinese nation and the Chinese civilization. In the course of the five thousand years of Chinese history, for more than three thousand years it served as the political, economic and cultural center of the country and therefore, as generally accepted, represents half of the history of China. Henan is the native place of Yellow Emperor, the cradle of Chinese culture, the starting point of the ancient Silk Road in the east, and the birthplace of Shaolin Kungfu and Chen-style Taijiquan—typical examples of the world-renowned Chinese martial arts. It was here that the earliest capital city in China was founded, the oldest Chinese characters engraved, and the earliest commerce took shape.

In the new era, Henan has witnessed rapid growth in its economy and remarkable improvement of people's living conditions, owing to the national reform and opening-up policy and unremitting endeavoring of the people. Modern economic achievements and social development as well as the changes of way of life could be traced back to its traditional values and cultural heritages. To enable people from other countries to understand Henan, and let the province integrate more efficiently into the world development, the Foreign Affairs Office of the People's Government of Henan Province, has organized teams of authoritative experts and scholars in relevant fields to compile this *Chinese Civilization: Stories from Henan* in Chinese and other foreign languages since 2018, by crystallizing the excellence of traditions and outstanding features of modern development. The book series include *Shaolin Kungfu, Taijiquan, Traditional Chinese Medicine, Chinese Characters, Cultural Heritage, A Model Official — Jiao Yulu, Man-made River — Hongqiqu Canal, the Silk*

*Road*, *Ancient Chinese Capitals*, *Handicraft* and *Feeding the People — Agriculture*, etc, attempting to present a panoramic picture of the province.

In today's world, human civilization has made great progress in both material accumulation and cultural and ethical advancement, and the great abundance of materials today, especially, is beyond the imagination of the ancient people. At the same time, however, modern people are also confronted with a lot of problems, such as the widening gap between the rich and the poor, the indulgence in pursuit of luxury and extravagance, the undesirable extension of individualism, the decline of social integrity, and the increasing tension between man and nature. To solve these problems, we need to draw on the wisdom and powers developed today as well as those accumulated in the past. Henan is endowed with a rich historical and cultural heritage characterized by its inclusiveness, and such a heritage remains significant today. The intelligence and wisdom in Henan culture are conducive to self-cultivation and to the promotion of social development. The spirit of serving the people and relentless struggle, as embodied in Jiao Yulu and Hongqiqu Canal, provides source of strength for building a community with a shared future for mankind. It is our hope that, wisdom and strength from Henan stories, could lead us to a shared brilliant future.

# 前 言

太极拳是极富中国传统民族特色元素的文化形态。

太极拳是中华民族辩证的理论思维与武术、艺术、导引术、中医等的完美结合，它以中国传统儒、道哲学中的太极、阴阳辩证理念为核心思想，集颐养性情、强身健体、技击对抗等多种功能为一体，是高层次的人体文化。作为一种饱含东方包容理念的运动形式，其习练者针对意、气、形、神的锻炼，非常符合人体生理和心理的要求，对人类个体身心健康以及人类群体的和谐共处，有着极为重要的促进作用。太极拳这种以体育运动作为主要外在表现形式和载体的非物质文化形态，充分体现了人类对自然界的客观认知和科学实践。

太极拳发源地中国河南省温县陈家沟太极拳集体演练活动
A Group Performance of Taijiquan in Chenjiagou Village

17世纪中叶，温县陈家沟村陈氏第9世陈王廷在家传拳法的基础上，吸收众家武术之长，融合易学、中医等思想，创编出一套具有阴阳开合、刚柔相济、内外兼修的新拳法，命名太极拳。陈王廷被后人尊为太极拳始祖。

太极拳在中国河南省温县陈家沟村陈氏家族世代传承，到了晚于陈王廷五代的陈长兴和陈有本，二人由博归约，分别创编出太极拳大架一路、二路和太极拳小架一路、二路。陈长兴从理论上对太极拳进行总结，著有《太极拳十大要论》《太极拳用武要言》《太极拳战斗篇》等。

太极拳从陈长兴起开始向族外传播。陈长兴传外姓弟子河北永年人杨露禅。杨露禅学成回乡，后到北京传拳，逐渐衍变，形成杨氏太极拳。陈家沟陈清平传拳于河北永年人武禹襄和温县赵堡村人和兆元、陈新庄人李景炎、南张羌村人李作智、北冷村人王赐信，后五人分别形成武氏太极拳、和氏太极拳、忽雷太极拳、腾挪太极拳和忽灵太极拳。北京大兴人全佑师从杨家学杨氏太极拳后，传子吴鉴泉，形成吴氏太极拳。河北武清（今属天津市）人李瑞东跟随杨露禅弟子王兰亭学杨氏太极拳后，形成李氏太极拳。河北完县（今顺平县）人孙禄堂师从郝为真学武氏太极拳后，形成孙氏太极拳。河北任县人王其和师从郝为真学习武氏太极拳，师从杨澄甫学习杨氏太极拳，融合贯通，自成一家，形成王其和太极拳。20世纪50年代，温县陈家沟人陈发科在祖传拳械套路的基础上，形成陈氏太极拳新架。

自陈长兴传拳杨露禅起，太极拳也从温县陈家沟一隅开始向全国和全世界传播开来。

太极拳基于太极阴阳理念，用意念统领全身，通过入静放松、以意导气、以气催形的反复习练，以进入妙手一运一太极、太极一运化乌有的境界，达到修身养性、陶冶情操、强身健体、益寿延年的目的。

太极拳含蓄内敛、连绵不断、以柔克刚、急缓相间、行云流水的拳术风格，是习练者的意、气、形、神逐渐趋于圆融一体的至高境界，而其对于武德修养的要求也使得习练者在增强体质的同时提高自身素养，促进人与自然、人与社会的融洽与和谐。

太极拳基本内容包括养生理论、拳术套路、器械套路、推手以及辅助训练法。

# Preface

Taijiquan is a cultural form which is rich in traditional Chinese characteristics.

Taijiquan is the perfect combination of Chinese dialectical theoretical thinking and martial arts, arts, *daoyin*, and traditional Chinese medicine. It is a high-level expression of human culture. It takes the dialectical ideas of Taiji, yin and yang of Confucianism and Daoism as its core idea. Furthermore, it combines the functions of temperament cultivation, physical exercise and martial confrontation. As a form of exercise, it involves the concept of oriental inclusiveness, whereby its practitioners exercise in intention, *qi,* form and spirit. It also satisfies physical and mental demands, which, to some degree, promotes the harmonious coexistence of human beings. As an intangible cultural form, Taijiquan takes sports as its main external manifestation while reflecting the cognition and scientific practice of human beings in the natural world.

In the mid 17th century, Chen Wangting (1600-1680), one of the 9th generation descendants of Chen family in Chenjiagou Village, Wenxian County, created a new boxing style called Taijiquan by absorbing other martial arts, the ideas of Yi (changes) and traditional Chinese medicine. The new boxing style was characterized by yin and yang, opening and closing, balance between hardness and softness, and combination of both inner and outer cultivation. Therefore, Chen Wangting was honored as the founder of Taijiquan.

From then on, Taijiquan was passed down from generation to generation in the Chen family of Chenjiagou. When it came to Chen Changxing (1771-1853) and Chen Youben (1780-1858), the 14th generation descendants, they created Routine One and Routine Two of the Big Frame and Routine One and Routine Two of the Small Frame respectively. In addition, Chen Changxing also theorized about Taijiquan, leaving his manuscript called *Ten Essentials of Taijiquan*, *Key Points of Taijiquan*, and *The Chapter on Fighting of Taijiquan*.

Afterwards, Chen style Taijiquan was taught to members of other families by Chen Changxing. One example was Yang Luchan of Yongnian, Hebei Province. After acquiring the skills of Taijiquan, Yang Luchan went to Beijing to teach boxing which gradually evolved into Yang style Taijiquan. Later, Chen Qingping in Chenjiagou Village taught the skills of Taijiquan to Wu Yuxiang from Yongnian, Hebei Province, He Zhaoyuan from Zhaobao Village, Li Jingyan from Chenxinzhuang Village, Li Zuozhi from Nanzhangqiang Village and Wang Cixin from Beileng Village, Wenxian County. With the efforts of the five disciples, Taijiquan evolved into Wu style, He style, Hulei style, Tengnuo style and Huling style respectively. Quan You from Daxing of Beijing passed on the skills of Taijiquan to his son Wu Jianquan after he learned Yang style and later it evolved into Wu style. Li Ruidong from Wuqing of Hebei Province learned Yang style Taijiquan from Wang Lanting, a disciple of Yang Luchan. This style then evolved into Li style. In the beginning of the Republic of China, Sun Lutang from Wanxian County of Hebei Province learned Taijiquan from Hao Weizhen, which later evolved into Sun style. During the period of the Republic of China, Wang Qihe, from Renxian County, Hebei Province, learned Wu style from Hao Weizhen and Yang style from Yang Chengfu and integrated both styles into Wang Qihe style. In the 1950s, Chen Fake from Chenjiagou developed the New Frame of Chen style Taijiquan on the basis of Chen family routines of boxing and weapons.

Since Chen Changxing taught the art to Yang Luchan, Taijiquan has spread from Chenjiagou to the entire China and even to the rest of the world.

Taijiquan is based on the concepts of yin and yang of the Taiji philosophy. Its practitioners, by employing the intention to direct the whole body, relax and produce *qi* through the intention and make the form through *qi*. This practice of Taijiquan is done repeatedly to reach the highest realm of self-cultivation, physical fitness and longevity.

Taijiquan has the features of implicitness and restraint, incessancy and continuity, overcoming hardness with softness, alternation of quickness and slowness, and naturalness and smoothness, which is the supreme realm of the practitioners in intention, *qi,* form and spirit. In regard to martial cultivation, Taijiquan enables its practitioners to enhance their physical fitness, their sense of accomplishment, and the harmony between themselves and nature, as well as society.

The main contents of Taijiquan include the theory of health preservation, boxing routines, weapon routines, pushing hands and auxiliary training methods.

# 目录　　　　　　　　　　　　　　　　　　　　Contents

第一章　太极拳的发源与传承　　　　　　　　　　001
Chapter Ⅰ　The Origin and Lineage of Taijiquan　　001

第二章　太极拳的理论体系　　　　　　　　　　　043
　　一、以心行气，以气运身，用意不用力　　　044
　　二、身肢放长，周身弹性　　　　　　　　　048
　　三、螺旋的顺逆缠丝劲　　　　　　　　　　050
　　四、虚实转换得当　　　　　　　　　　　　052
　　五、节节贯串　　　　　　　　　　　　　　052
　　六、一气呵成　　　　　　　　　　　　　　054
　　七、刚柔相济　　　　　　　　　　　　　　056
　　八、快慢相间　　　　　　　　　　　　　　058

Chapter Ⅱ　The Theoretical System of Taijiquan　　043
　　Ⅰ. Control *Qi* by Mind, Move the Body by *Qi*, and Focus on Intention Rather than Force　　045
　　Ⅱ. Stretch Out the Body and Make Flexible Movements　　049
　　Ⅲ. Start a Silk-Reeling *Jin*　　051
　　Ⅳ. Shift Emptiness and Fullness Appropriately　　053
　　Ⅴ. Coordinate Every Part of the Body　　055
　　Ⅵ. Move Smoothly Without Pause　　057
　　Ⅶ. Keep the Balance between Hardness and Softness　　057
　　Ⅷ. Alternate with Quickness and Slowness　　059

第三章　太极拳的技术体系　　　　　　　　　　　061
　　一、太极拳的五种步法和太极五步劲别　　　062

二、太极拳的八门劲别和太极八法　　　　　　　　　　068

Chapter Ⅲ　The Technical System of Taijiquan　　　　　　　061
  Ⅰ. The Five Footwork Methods and Their Corresponding Types
   of *Jin* of Taijiquan　　　　　　　　　　　　　　　　063
  Ⅱ. Taijiquan's Eight Types of *Jin* and Eight Techniques　　071

**第四章　太极拳的价值体系**　　　　　　　　　　　　　　077
  一、太极拳的技击价值　　　　　　　　　　　　　　078
  二、太极拳的养生价值　　　　　　　　　　　　　　080
  三、太极拳的社会价值　　　　　　　　　　　　　　082

Chapter Ⅳ　Functions and Values of Taijiquan　　　　　　　077
  Ⅰ. The Combat Value of Taijiquan　　　　　　　　　079
  Ⅱ. Health Preservation Value of Taijiquan　　　　　　079
  Ⅲ. The Social Value of Taijiquan　　　　　　　　　　081

**第五章　太极拳的未来发展**　　　　　　　　　　　　　　087
  一、太极拳未来在中国国内的传承发展　　　　　　　088
  二、太极拳未来在国际上的传承发展　　　　　　　　106

Chapter Ⅴ　The Future Development of Taijiquan　　　　　　087

Ⅰ. The Future Development of Taijiquan in China　089
Ⅱ. The Inheritance and Development of Taijiquan in the International Community　107

第六章　太极拳名家的故事　125
　　一、陈王廷校场比武　126
　　二、陈王廷防守黄河　128
　　三、陈王廷木门寨讨牛　132
　　四、陈王廷闷来造拳　136
　　五、陈所乐平皋纵子　140
　　六、太极天王双英破敌　142
　　七、巧妞失手陈门立规　146
　　八、陈敬柏神靠除霸　150
　　九、太极神肘陈继夏　154
　　十、陈公兆力斗疯牛　158

Chapter Ⅵ　Stories of Well-known Taijiquan Masters　125
　　Ⅰ. Chen Wangting Competing in Military Skills at a Drill Ground　127
　　Ⅱ. Chen Wangting Guarding along the Yellow River　129
　　Ⅲ. Chen Wangting Asking for the Lent Ox at Mumenzhai　133
　　Ⅳ. Chen Wangting Creating Taijiquan　137
　　Ⅴ. Chen Suole Spoiling His Sons in Pinggao　141
　　Ⅵ. Twin Brothers Capturing Bandits　145

Ⅶ. Chen Family Setting a Rule after Chen Qiaoniu Killed a Bully　　149
Ⅷ. Chen Jingbai Killing a Bully by His Powerful Shouldering　　153
Ⅸ. Chen Jixia, Well-known for His Elbowing　　157
Ⅹ. Chen Gongzhao Fighting against a Bull　　161

后　　记　　164
Postscript　　165

附录一　中国历史年代简表　　168
Appendix Ⅰ　A Brief Chronology of Chinese History　　168

附录二　专用词表（汉英）　　171
Appendix Ⅱ　Glossary (Chinese-English)　　171

第一章

# 太极拳的发源与传承

## Chapter I

## The Origin and Lineage of Taijiquan

太极拳，发源于中国河南省温县陈家沟村。

太极拳发源地——中国河南省温县陈家沟村貌
Panorama of Chenjiagou Village, the Birthplace of Taijiquan

温县陈家沟村位于黄河北岸，温县城东5公里的清风岭上，地理坐标北纬34°56′33″，东经113°8′40″（以陈氏太极拳祖祠正门为坐标点）。它北负太行之雄，南据虎牢之险，有黄河天堑为屏，在冷兵器时代，这里历来就是兵家必争之地。武王伐纣、楚汉之争、虎牢关之战等著名古代战役也都发生在此，所以这里的人们自古尚武。陈家沟与伏羲画卦台隔河相望，有着厚重的太极文化的积淀。它与神农涧相距不远，又是著名的怀药之乡，中医、中药文化在此根深蒂固，是闻名中外的太极拳发源地、中国太极拳文化研究基地、省级生态文明村。

陈家沟全村面积2万余平方米，共有10个村民小组，700多户，2800余人（常住人口3000余人），陈姓约占总人口的70%。

陈家沟村南有隔黄河相望的虎牢关、伏羲台、河洛文化等遗址。虎牢关是东控开封、西扼洛阳两都的军事要塞。在伊洛河与黄河交汇处，一清一浊两股河水形成了天然太极图。伏羲台是当年伏羲登高俯瞰黄河与洛水相交，构思孕育太极图的地方，是"易文化"的发源地。距陈家沟西北不远处有道教圣地沁阳市二仙庙，西南100公里处有少林寺，道教文化、佛教文化与儒教文化在这里汇集，形成了推动中华文明发展的

Taijiquan originated from the village of Chenjiagou, Wenxian County, Henan Province, China.

The village (34°56'33″ N, 113°8'40″ E) is located on the Qingfeng Ridge, five kilometers to the east of the county town. Contained by the Taihang Mountain in the north and the Yellow River to the south, the strategic region was a famous battlefield in ancient China. Therefore, martial arts have been honored here. In addition, Chenjiagou has been greatly influenced by Taiji culture and traditional Chinese medicine (TCM) culture. Across the Yellow River is where Fuxi, a legendary Chinese ancestor, created Eight Trigrams and the village is home to the well-known Huai herbal medicines. Nowadays, Chenjiagou has become an international research center for Taijiquan culture as well as an ecological village.

It covers an area of over 20,000 square meters, with a total population of about 3,000 from 700 households, among which 70% are of the Chen family.

There are many cultural heritage sites related to the origin of Taijiquan around Chenjiagou. Across the Yellow River, there are some ancient cultural sites, including the Hulao Pass, the Terrace where Fuxi created Eight Trigrams, etc. The Hulao Pass was a military pass that could dominate the two important cities of Kaifeng to the east and Luoyang to the west. The Terrace where Fuxi created Eight Trigrams was where the culture of *Zhou Yi (The Book of Changes)* originated. Fuxi proposed Taiji Eight Trigrams when he saw the natural yin-yang diagram formed by the turbid water and the clear water where the Yellow River and the Yiluo River met. To the northwest of Chenjiagou is a Daoist site named the Erxian Temple in Qinyang City, and a hundred kilometers to the southwest is the Shaolin Temple. With Daoism, Buddhism and Confucianism converging, the Central Plains culture developed and subsequently promoted the development of Chinese civilization. The unique cultural and geographical environment had a far-reaching impact on the creator of Taijiquan, Chen Wangting.

In late Yuan dynasty (1271-1368), Zhu Yuanzhang, the leader of a peasant uprising, sent troops to cross the Yellow River to conquer north China. This begun a long-term war between the Yuan troops and the rebellious troops in Huaiqing Prefecture (Now it is Qinyang City of Henan Province) on the north bank of the Yellow River. The war, coupled with natural disasters, turned the surrounding fertile region into an untamed area with almost no residents.

厚重的中原文化。这里特殊的人文地理环境和厚重的中华传统文化对明末清初陈王廷创编太极拳产生了深远影响。

太极拳发源地——中国河南省温县陈家沟村口牌坊
The Memorial Archway in Chenjiagou Village

元朝末年,农民起义领袖朱元璋派兵北伐,强渡黄河,与元军在黄河北岸怀庆府(今沁阳)属地长期交战。战争和自然灾害使怀庆府方圆数百里人烟几绝,良田荒芜。

明洪武五年(1372),朱元璋下令以山西洪洞县为中心向怀庆府属地移民。祖籍泽州(今晋城)东土河村的青年陈卜,逃荒到洪洞县,与家人一起被裹入移民队伍进入怀庆府境内,辗转流离,最终落脚常阳村。此村位于清风岭上,南临黄河,旱涝保收。随着陈氏家族人丁繁衍兴旺,清初常阳村易名陈家沟。

明初陈氏始祖陈卜定居于此后,勤劳耕作,兴家立业。为了保卫桑梓不受匪盗危害,精通拳械的陈卜在村中设立武学社,传授子孙习拳练武,村民习武成风。

In 1372, Zhu Yuanzhang, the first emperor of the Ming dynasty (1368-1644), ordered the residents in Hongtong County of Shanxi to migrant to Huaiqing Prefecture. Suffering from successive disasters at his hometown, Dongtuhe Village, Zezhou, Shanxi, a young man named Chen Bu and his family members fled from famine to Hongtong County and were taken with other migrants to Huaiqing. After running away from place to place, they settled down at Changyang Village, which is located on the Qingfeng Ridge. It is to the north of the Yellow River with the favorable climate. With the prosperity of the Chen family, Changyang Village was changed to Chenjiagou Village in early Qing dynasty.

After settling down in Chenjiagou Village, they worked hard and their family became prosperous. In order to protect them from banditry, Chen Bu, who was proficient in boxing, set up a martial arts school in the village to teach his descendants. And boxing practice became popular among the villagers.

Chen Wangting (1600-1680), with the courtesy name Zouting, was one of the 9th generation descendants of Chen Bu in Chenjiagou, Wenxian County, Henan Province in late Ming and early Qing dynasties. Both his father Chen Fumin and his grandfather Chen Sigui loved martial arts very much. Since his childhood, he had been deeply influenced by the traditional Chinese culture and he was well accomplished with both the pen and the sword. In his young adulthood, he once served as a security guard in armor on many journeys in Henan, Shandong and Shanxi, and consequently established a good reputation. However, when the reign of Ming dynasty was over and the whole country was thrown into chaos, he was very disappointed with this new harsh reality. He then decided to live in the countryside, and devoted much of his study to folk martial arts with the company of *Huang Ting Jing (The Yellow Court Classic)*. Then during the time from the year 1650 to 1680, based on the martial arts passed on within his clan, he integrated other various schools of martial arts and created a completely new routine.

The martial art created by Chen Wangting is rooted in Taiji, one of the essential parts of the traditional Chinese culture, taking in the idea of harmony between man and nature and the theory of yin and yang, and integrates other schools of martial arts, the meridian theory of the traditional Chinese medicine, and the techniques of *daoyin* and breathing of Daoism. It is none other than the

陈王廷（1600—1680），字奏庭，明末清初河南温县陈家沟村人，陈卜第九代孙，祖父陈思贵，父陈抚民，均好拳习武。陈王廷自幼受中原文化熏陶，擅长拳法，文武兼备。青年时披坚执锐，在河南、山东、山西一带走镖征战，负有盛名。明朝覆灭后的一段时期，时局动荡。面对冷酷的现实，陈王廷报国无门，万念俱灰，郁郁而不得志。晚年，他隐居乡里，以《黄庭经》为伴，潜心收集、研究民间武术。在家传拳术的基础上，陈王廷将众家武术之长融汇合成，加上自己平生习武所悟，在1650年至1680年间，创编了一种全新的武术体系。

陈王廷创编的武术体系，理根太极，秉承中国传统的"天人合一"思想和阴阳生克之理，汲取诸家武术之长，融中医经络学与道家导引吐纳术为一体。这种刚柔相济、阴阳互化、变幻莫测、威力无比的武术拳种就是"太极拳"。

陈王廷创编太极拳之后，主要在陈氏家族内传播，代表性人物有族侄陈家沟陈氏第十世陈所乐和陈汝信。他们都是太极拳的第二代传人。

陈所乐（1625—1704）师承太极拳始祖陈王廷。其故宅遗址与后来杨露禅学拳的陈德瑚宅院对门。因家境富裕，有时虽应朋友之邀跑趟镖事，但他并不以此为生。平日在村中设帐授徒，陈氏子弟从其学武者甚多，主要有侄儿陈光印、陈正如和孪生子陈恂如、陈申如等。

陈汝信（1630—1711）师承太极拳始祖陈王廷。他勤学苦练，功夫日臻炉火纯青，深得陈王廷喜爱。其子陈大鲲、陈大鹏皆得其真传而名满江湖。

太极拳第三代代表性传承人主要有陈恂如、陈申如、陈正如等。

陈恂如（1635—1655）、陈申如（1635—1715），陈家沟陈氏第十一世，陈所乐之孪生子，自幼随父习拳。兄弟二人是太极拳史上具有传奇色彩的人物，年未弱冠而拳术精湛。幼年见义勇为，以高超拳术斗群匪解邻村北平皋王家之围，被誉为"大天神、二天神"。王家特将二人大德编为戏曲传唱，名曰"双英破敌"。

well-known "Taijiquan", which has features such as balance between hardness and softness, transformation between yin and yang, unpredictable changes of movements and incomparable attacking and defending power.

太极拳创始人陈王廷画像
Portrait of Chen Wangting, the Founder of Taijiquan

Chen Wangting began to spread Taijiquan within his own family. The major representatives are Chen Wangting's nephews, the 10th generation descendants Chen Suole and Chen Ruxin, who are the 2nd generation lineage holders of Taijiquan.

Chen Suole (1625-1704) learned Taijiquan from Chen Wangting, the founder of Taijiquan. His former residence is opposite of Chen Dehu's, where Yang Luchan learned Taijiquan. Sometimes Chen Suole was asked by his friends to be a security guard on some journeys, but he did not make a living by it because of his wealthy family. Usually he stayed in the village and taught Taijiquan for those who were interested in martial arts. Many of those came from Chen family, among whom his nephews Chen Guangyin and Chen Zhengru and also his twin sons Chen Xunru and Chen Shenru were the most outstanding.

Chen Ruxin (1630-1711) also learned Taijiquan from Chen Wangting. He worked very hard in acquisition of Taijiquan, and gradually grew into a highly-skilled master loved much by Chen Wangting. His sons Chen Dakun and Chen Dapeng learned a lot from him and were both well-known by ordinary people.

陈正如（1650—1730），陈家沟陈氏第十一世，师承陈所乐，精于一百单八势太极长拳。陈正如教子从严，授徒有方，其弟子陈敬柏、郭永福，其子陈廉、陈爵、陈义、陈静等皆以文韬武略闻名于世。

太极拳第四代代表性传承人主要有陈敬柏、陈继夏等。

陈敬柏，又名基，陈家沟陈氏第十二世。拳艺出神入化而擅长用靠。年轻时曾从巡抚于鲁，晚年归隐乡里。一日，赴县城东关，见一卖艺者王定国口出狂言，遂以奇技胜之。谁知此人怀恨在心，三年后复至陈家沟寻衅。时陈敬柏已年逾八旬，再三谦让，而对方不允，竟连下毒手。陈敬柏忍无可忍，一个迎门靠，将对方打在石碑上，碑断人亡。陈敬柏回家后亦即病倒，数日后谢世。至今民间流传着"打死王定国，累死陈敬柏"的故事。

太极拳第四代代表性传承人陈敬柏画像
Portrait of Chen Jingbai, one of the Representatives of the 4th Generation of Taijiquan Successors

陈继夏，字炳南，陈家沟陈氏第十二世。师承族叔陈光印学太极拳，善肘。以磨面为生，借推磨练内劲。平日善用肘，与陈敬柏齐名，有"陈继夏肘，陈敬柏靠"之称。除武功外，善丹青，每画俱能

Major representatives of the 3rd generation lineage holders of Taijiquan are Chen Xunru, Chen Shenru and Chen Zhengru.

Chen Xunru (1635-1655) and Chen Shenru (1635-1715), who are of the 11th generation descendants of Chen family of Chenjiagou and the twin sons of Chen Suole, learned Taijiquan from their father since childhood. The two brothers were legendary figures in the history of Taijiquan. They had been very good at martial arts before adulthood. Additionally, they were once praised as "the elder hero" and "the younger hero" when they defeated a group of bandits by using their excellent skills and went on to rescue the Wang family from a siege. Deeply moved by the great virtue of the two brothers, the Wang family made that special event into a drama, called *Twin Brothers Capturing Bandits*.

Chen Zhengru (1650-1730), one of the 11th generation descendants of Chen family of Chenjiagou, was instructed by Chen Suole and skilled in the 108-form routine of Taijiquan. He was very strict and skillful in the instruction of his disciples, many of whom, such as Chen Jingbai, Guo Yongfu, and his sons Chen Lian, Chen Jue, Chen Yi and Chen Jing, were world-renowned for their civil and military skills.

Major representatives of the 4th generation lineage holders of Taijiquan are Chen Jingbai and Chen Jixia.

Chen Jingbai, also named Ji, is of the 12th generation descendants of Chen family in Chenjiagou. He was very skilled in the martial arts and was especially good at using his shoulders. He was a policeman in Shandong Province, and returned to his home place in later years. One day, he came across an entertainer, who showed off the martial arts in public to make a living. When he found that the man was bragging too much about his own martial arts, he challenged him to a competition which he won by using his excellent skills. However, no one knew that the man harbored a grudge and returned to Chenjiagou to make trouble three years later. At that time, Chen was more than eighty years old, and although he had tried to be humble and tolerant, the man did not make the slightest concession and thus struck vicious blows relentlessly. Finally, Chen could not bear any more and struck him against a stone tablet by using the shoulders, which broke off the tablet and killed the man. After he returned home, he fell ill and died several days later. Even to this day the story of how "Chen Jingbai was too

传神入妙。

太极拳第五代代表性传承人主要有陈公兆、陈秉奇、陈秉壬、陈秉旺等。

陈公兆（1715—1810），字德基，陈家沟陈氏第十三世。乾隆六十年（1795），陈家沟85岁的陈善和88岁的陈毓英奉旨至京赴"千叟宴"。返乡时巡抚、知府为二叟挂匾。不料鞭炮惊牛直冲人群而来，绿营兵将不知所措。时陈公兆80岁，力斗惊牛，将牛掀翻在地，巡抚、知府、绿营兵将和围观群众无不钦仰。至今，陈家沟还流传着他的"养生歌诀"："三十年不停拳，三十年不饱饭，三十年独自乐，三十年独自眠。"

陈秉奇、陈秉壬、陈秉旺，三人是堂兄弟，明嘉靖年间人。陈家沟陈氏第十三世。三人从小拜族叔陈继夏为师，学习家传太极拳术。五年扎基功夫过后，陈继夏便将三人分开，分别授予技击、点穴、卸骨绝技。兄弟三人得真传后，又互相切磋琢磨，个个艺精入神，方圆百里，无人不知，谓之"陈氏三雄"。秉壬除武功外，更兼精医术，为人和善，助人为乐，教子有方。后三人将拳技尽传于秉旺之子长兴。

太极拳第六代代表性传承人主要有太极长拳主要传人郭永福、太极拳大架创编人陈长兴、太极拳小架创编人陈有本等。

郭永福（1736—1796），本名陈有孚，陈家沟陈氏第十四世，其父陈永兆，母亲郭氏。因其在温县打死一名恶霸，于1770年逃往山西省洪洞县苏堡镇，改名郭永福。郭永福擅长太极长拳，亲传弟子主要有山西的贺怀璧、张秀德。

exhausted and died after killing a martial arts entertainer from Shandong" is still repeatedly told among people.

Chen Jixia, with the courtesy name Bingnan, is of the 12th generation descendants of Chen family in Chenjiagou. He learned to practice Taijiquan from his uncle Chen Guangyin and was good at using his elbows. With a poor family, he lived mainly by grinding flour and practiced the inner force by moving the stone mill. Because he was skillful in using elbows, he got the same reputation with Chen Jingbai, who was good at using shoulders. Besides the martial arts, Chen Jixia was still good at painting.

Major representatives of the 5th generation lineage holders of Taijiquan are Chen Gongzhao, Chen Bingqi, Chen Bingren and Chen Bingwang.

Chen Gongzhao (1715-1810), with the courtesy name Deji, is of the 13th generation descendants of Chen family in Chenjiagou. In the 60th year of the reign of the Emperor Qianlong (1795), in order to show the prosperity of Qing dynasty and advocate the good practice of respecting the old, the imperial court invited all people over 80 years old with virtues and talents to attend the "one thousand old men banquet" in the Taihe Palace of the capital. Chen Shan, 85 years old at that time and the 12th generation descendant of Chen family in Chenjiagou, along with Chen Yuying, 88 years old, the 13th generation descendant of Chen family, was invited to take part in the banquet. After returning home, the province governor and the city magistrate held a special plaque ceremony for the two that attracted a large audience. Unexpectedly, a scared bull ran straight towards the audience. The people on the scene including the guard soldiers were suddenly at a loss. Luckily Chen Gongzhao, 80 years old at that time, fought against the scared bull and finally threw it to the ground. This incredible act won the great admiration of the governor, the magistrate, the soldiers and all of the ordinary onlookers, who repeatedly exclaimed: "What a brilliant man!" In addition, even to this day his ideas of keeping healthy are still very popular among the people in Chenjiagou, such as "insisting on Taijiquan practice for 30 years", "keeping a good diet for 30 years", "maintaining a good mood for 30 years" and "sleeping alone without sex for 30 years".

Chen Bingqi, Chen Bingren and Chen Bingwang, the 13th generation descendants of Chen family in Chenjiagou, are cousins who learned to practice

太极拳第六代代表性传承人陈长兴画像

Portrait of Chen Changxing, One of the Representatives of the 6th Generation of Taijiquan Successors

陈长兴（1771—1853），字云亭，陈家沟陈氏第十四世。秉承家学，功夫深厚，练拳行走身正合一，人称"牌位先生"。他在陈王廷所传套路基础上，精练归纳，衍变出今日流传的陈氏太极拳大架一路和二路（又名炮捶）。其弟子最著者有陈耕耘、杨露禅。

陈有本（1780—1858），陈家沟陈氏第十四世。他在陈王廷所传套路的基础上，精益求精，创编了一套以走立圆、走小圈为主的套路，世人称之为"陈氏太极拳小架"。陈氏太极拳小架师承严格，多在陈氏族内传授，鲜为人知，普及范围有限。

Taijiquan from their uncle Chen Jixia. After five years of basic training, Chen Jixia separated the three, and imparted three unique skills to them respectively, namely skilled attacking, hitting vital points, and breaking bones. When they mastered the skills, they exchanged ideas with each other and each of them was very skilled in the martial arts. They were well-known as "the three heroes". Chen Bingren was not only good at the martial arts, but also did quite well in medical treatment. Besides, he was very kind, ready to help others in need, and was a qualified parent in child's education. Later on, the three brothers passed all their martial arts to Chen Changxing, the son of Chen Bingwang.

Major representatives of the 6th generation lineage holders of Taijiquan are Guo Yongfu, the major lineage holder of Taiji Changquan, Chen Changxing, the creator of the Big Frame of Taijiquan, and Chen Youben, the creator of the Small Frame of Taijiquan.

Guo Yongfu (1736-1796), with the original name Chen Youfu, is of the 14th generation descendants of Chen family in Chenjiagou. His father is Chen Yongzhao and his mother's family name is Guo. Because he killed a bully in Wenxian County and fled to Subao Town, Hongdong County, Shanxi Province in 1770, he changed his name to Guo Yongfu. He was good at using Taiji Changquan and his disciples included He Huaibi and Zhang Xiude in Shanxi Province.

Chen Changxing (1771-1853), with the courtesy name Yunting, is of the 14th generation descendants of Chen family in Chenjiagou. He began to learn Taijiquan from his father Chen Bingwang since childhood. Because of his talents in martial arts and his integrity, he was called as "the qualified teacher" in the martial arts. On the basis of the routines learned from Chen Wangting, he created the new complete routines, Routine One and Routine Two of the Big Frame, which are popular nowadays. He had many disciples, among whom the most well-known were Chen Gengyun and Yang Luchan.

Chen Youben (1780-1858) is of the 14th generation descendants of Chen family in Chenjiagou. On the basis of the routines instructed by Chen Wangting, he studied the Taijiquan theories with greater efforts and created a new routine of Taijiquan with a quite different style focusing on making small rather than big circle movements, which was called the Small Frame of Taijiquan. The Small

太极拳第六代代表性传承人陈有本画像

Portrait of Chen Youben, One of the Representatives of the 6th Generation of Taijiquan Successors

陈氏太极拳第七代代表性传承人主要有陈清平、陈耕耘、陈仲甡、陈季甡、杨露禅等。

陈清平（1795—1868），陈家沟陈氏第十五世，陈有本族侄，居住在陈家沟北二公里的赵堡村。自幼随陈有本习练太极拳小架，结合自己的心得体会，形成与师陈有本不同的太极拳小架套路。人们称其师小架为"略"，称其小架为"圈"。陈清平太极拳与陈家沟所传在架形上有明显不同。因其于赵堡村开馆授徒，后人称其所传拳架为赵堡太极拳或太极拳赵堡架。赵堡拳架注重开合与轻灵，陈沟拳架注重沉稳与缠丝。赵堡太极拳在其后的一百多年里，枝繁叶茂，名手辈出，主要分布在河南温县的赵堡镇、张羌街道、北冷乡与河北邯郸市永年区。

陈清平的弟子中，和兆元、牛发虎、张汉、李景炎、李作智、武禹襄、任长春、陈景阳、王赐信等最为著名，对太极拳的发展都作出了一定贡献。赵堡村人和兆元创"代理架"，又称"赵堡快架"，即和氏太极拳；辛堂村人李景炎创"忽颤架"，即忽雷太极拳；南张羌村人李作智创"权托架"，又称"矮桩架"，即腾挪太极拳；河北永年人武禹襄

Frame of Taijiquan was strictly taught in the Chen family and, therefore, was not popular among people.

Major representatives of the 7th generation lineage holders of Taijiquan are Chen Qingping, Chen Gengyun, Chen Zhongshen, Chen Jishen and Yang Luchan.

Chen Qingping (1795-1868), the nephew of Chen Youben, is of the 15th generation descendants of Chen family in Chenjiagou, who lived in Zhaobao Village two kilometers north of Chenjiagou. He learned to practice the Small Frame of Taijiquan from his uncle Chen Youben since his childhood, and made some improvements. And the small Frame created by him was called "circle", and the one created by his uncle Chen Youben, "Lüe". Because of the differences between his style and Chenjiagou style and the different places, his style was called Zhaobao style or Zhaobao Taijiquan. Zhaobao style focused on opening and closing, and Chen style focused on stability and the spiral force. For more than one hundred years, Zhaobao Taijiquan has developed and trained many disciples in Zhaobao Town, Zhangqiang Street and Beileng Town, Wenxian County, Henan Province and Yongnian, Handan City, Hebei Province.

Among Chen Qingping's disciples, the most famous ones included He Zhaoyuan, Niu Fahu, Zhang Han, Li Jingyan, Li Zuozhi, Wu Yuxiang, Ren Changchun, Chen Jingyang, Wang Cixin and the others, who have contributed to the development of Taijiquan. He Zhaoyuan from Zhaobao Village created He style Taijiquan. Li Jingyan from Xintang Village created Hulei style Taijiquan. Li Zuozhi from Nanzhangqiang Village created Tengnuo style Taijiquan. Wu Yuxiang from Yongnian, Hebei Province created Wu style Taijiquan. Wang Cixin from Beileng Village created Huling style Taijiquan. Ren Changchun from Xixinzhuang Village created Lingluo style Taijiquan. Sun Lutang instructed by Wu Yuxiang created Sun style Taijiquan. From the above styles of Taijiquan, it is obvious that Chen Qingping has made an indelible contribution to the spread and development of Taijiquan.

Chen Gengyun, with the courtesy name Xiacun, is of the 15th generation descendants of Chen family in Chenjiagou and the son of Chen Changxing. He learned to practice Taijiquan from his father since he was young and became outstanding among his peers. He worked as a security guard commuting to

创武氏太极拳；北冷村人王赐信创忽灵太极拳；西辛庄村人任长春创领落太极拳。武禹襄再传弟子孙禄堂创孙氏太极拳。陈清平为太极拳的传播、发展作出了不可磨灭的贡献。

太极拳第七代代表性传承人陈清平画像

Portrait of Chen Qingping, One of the Representatives of the 7th Generation of Taijiquan Successors

陈耕耘，字霞村，陈家沟陈氏第十五世，陈长兴之子。从小习练家传太极拳，青年时已成名手，在同辈中出类拔萃。走镖山东，以惊人技艺威震贼胆。光绪年间，山东莱州府百姓为其立碑曰："数年来，莱州地界盗贼蜂起，打家劫舍，强抢民财。来往客商，黎民百姓，深受其害，苦不堪言。虽官军屡次剿捕，收效甚微。幸有豫省陈家沟拳师陈公耕耘，保镖到此，只身闯入贼巢，舍命拼杀，力战贼魁，一举全歼。解百姓以倒悬，救商贾出苦海，可谓英雄虎胆，武功盖世。莱州各界士农工商，三教九流，感其大恩，无以为报，特聚敛银两，立碑记之，以传后世。"后袁世凯赴山东见碑，遣人来温请陈耕耘教子，时耕耘已故去多年，遂聘耕耘子延熙。

陈仲甡（1809—1871），字志曛，又字宜篪，号石厂，陈家沟陈氏

Shandong Province and frightened the bandits with his Taijiquan. In the reign of the Emperor Guangxu, people in Laizhou, Shandong Province set up a monument for him on which was recorded his heroic deeds. "For many years, the bandits and robbers always caused some trouble to the local people in Laizhou, Shandong Province and people and merchants there suffered a lot. Although the officers and soldiers tried to arrest them, the bandits and the robbers always slipped from their fingers. Fortunately, the master Chen Gengyun, as a security guard, came here and defeated all of them. It was a relief for all the local people and the merchants. Therefore, this monument was set up in memory of Chen." Later, Yuan Shikai, one of the famous politicians and militarists in the period of Northern Warlords, came to Shangdong and saw this monument. He sent his followers to Wenxian County to invite Chen Gengyun to teach his son Taijiquan. But Chen Gengyun had been dead for many years. So Chen Yanxi, the son of Chen Gengyun was invited to teach Yuan's son.

Chen Zhongshen (1809-1871), with the courtesy name Zhixun, is of the 15th generation descendants of Chen family in Chenjiagou. Chen Zhongshen and Chen Jishen were twin brothers and it was hard for the villagers to distinguish them. Chen Zhongshen was deeply influenced by his father Chen Youheng and his uncle Chen Youben and became proficient in Taijiquan. Later, he and his brother were admitted to the school. He was valiant and could use the iron spear that weighed about 15 kilograms.

Chen Jishen (1809-1865), with the courtesy name Fangsui, is of the 15th generation descendants of Chen family in Chenjiagou. Influenced by Chen Youheng and Chen Youben when he was young, he was determined to read books on history and strategy and to study martial arts. He was admitted to the school with his elder brother Chen Zhongshen. He emphasized etiquette, filial piety and friendship and had the same reputation as his brother Zhongshen.

Yang Luchan (1799-1872), also named Fukui, is from Yanmen, Yongnian County (Nowadays Yanmen belongs to Yongnian District, Handan City, Hebei Province), Guangping Prefecture, Zhili Province in the Qing dynasty. In the early 19th century, following Chen Dehu, the boss of Taihe Pharmacy in Guangping, Yang Luchan came to Chenjiagou, Wenxian County, Henan Province and learned to practice Taijiquan from Chen Changxing. After acquiring the skills

第十五世。仲甡、季甡系孪生兄弟，貌酷似，乡邻难辨。自幼深受父陈有恒、叔陈有本熏陶，韬略无不精通。少年与弟同入武庠，能使用和演练30斤左右的铁枪，聪颖过人，勇武敏捷。

陈季甡（1809—1865），字仿随，陈家沟陈氏第十五世。幼受父辈陈有恒、陈有本熏陶，立志涉经史，读兵书，钻研武学，少年即与兄陈仲甡同入武庠。平日重礼仪，守孝道，广交友，与兄仲甡齐名。

杨露禅（1799—1872），名福魁，字露禅，以字行世。清直隶省广平府永年县闫门寨（今河北省邯郸市永年区）人。19世纪初叶，杨露禅随广平府西大街药号太和堂东家陈德瑚至河南省怀庆府温县陈家沟，师从陈长兴学太极拳。艺成授拳京城，逐渐改编拳套动作，后经其子、孙一再修订，成为流行于世的杨氏太极拳。露禅拳艺传人主要有凌山、万春、全佑以及诸子。2006年5月20日，杨氏太极拳随陈氏太极拳一起入列第一批国家级非物质文化遗产名录。

太极拳第七代传承人中的大部分都只在陈家沟陈氏家族内传授太极拳，不以授拳为生。后唯有杨露禅到河北、北京等地，靠传授太极拳谋生，广收门徒。而陈清平经商之余，在赵堡开馆授徒。至此，太极拳才开始走出陈家沟，向外广为传播。

太极拳第八代代表性传承人主要有陈鑫、陈延熙、和兆元、武禹襄、李景炎、李作智、王赐信、任长春、杨健侯、杨班侯、李瑞东等。

陈鑫（1849—1929），字品三，河南省温县陈家沟人，清岁贡生，近代中国体育史、武术史上著名的太极拳家，太极拳理论集大成者。其著述有《陈氏太极拳图说》四卷、《太极拳引蒙入路》（即《陈氏太极拳图说》简明本）、《三三六拳谱》、《陈氏家乘》五卷、《安愚轩诗文集》若干卷等。陈鑫弟子主要有陈克孝、陈克弟、陈克忠、陈克信、陈克礼、陈克义、陈克强、陈克良等。

of Taijiquan, he came to Beijing and taught Taijiquan there. And on the basis of revisions and modifications from his sons and grandsons, his skills of Taijiquan developed into the Yang style Taijiquan which was still popular today. The major lineage holders of Yang Luchan included Lingshan, Wanchun, Quanyou and the others. On May 20, 2006, Yang style Taijiquan was listed in the first national intangible cultural heritage list with Chen style Taijiquan.

Among the 7th generation lineage holders of Taijiquan, most of them taught Taijiquan but not for a living and their disciples were limited to the Chen family, Chenjiagou. Later, it was Yang Luchan who taught Taijiquan for a living and enrolled many disciples in Hebei Province and Beijing. And Chen Qingping opened a martial club in Zhaobao and enrolled disciples since he ran a business. From then on, Taijiquan began to spread widely out of Chenjiagou.

太极拳第七代代表性传承人杨露禅画像
Portrait of Yang Luchan, One of the Representatives of the 7th Generation of Taijiquan Successors

Major representatives of the 8th generation of lineage holders of Taijiquan are Chen Xin, Chen Yanxi, He Zhaoyuan, Wu Yuxiang, Li Jingyan, Li Zuozhi, Wang Cixin, Ren Changchun, Yang Jianhou, Yang Banhou and Li Ruidong, ect.

Chen Xin (1849-1929), with the courtesy name Pinsan, is the native of Chenjiagou Village, Wenxian County, Henan Province. He was a senior licentiate in the Qing dynasty, a noted Taijiquan practitioner in the history of modern Chinese sports and the master of Taijiquan theory. His major works included *The*

太极拳第八代代表性传承人陈鑫画像
Portrait of Chen Xin, One of the Representatives of the 8th Generation of Taijiquan Successors

陈延熙（1848—1929），河南省温县陈家沟人，陈耕耘次子。自幼随父学拳。常夜卧条凳，醒即练拳不止。耕读之余，教习子弟练拳。光绪二十六年（1900），袁世凯督鲁，见乡人为陈耕耘所立碑记，知太极拳为陈氏专精，遂派人来访，意请陈耕耘授己子侄拳艺。时陈耕耘已逝，遂聘陈延熙前往。当时袁府各派武师，多有妒之者，经与之比较后，无不心服。延熙随袁自鲁而津，教授六年，以母老辞归。

和兆元（1810—1890），河南省温县赵堡人，出身中医世家。师承陈清平学太极拳，悉心苦练。后根据自己多年练拳体念，对师传拳架手法、身法、步法与姿势进行合理化修改，逐渐形成了一套架式，被称作"代理架"，现一般称和氏太极拳。和氏太极拳强调理法自然，称行功走架为"耍拳"。和兆元传子和润芝、和敬芝，孙和庆喜，徒苗彦生等。2014年11月11日，和氏太极拳入列第一批国家级非物质文化遗产扩展项目名录。

*Illustrated Canon of Chen Style Taijiquan* (4 volumes), *Introduction to Taijiquan*, *Boxing 336*, *On Chen Family*, and *Poetry Collection*. His representative disciples are Chen Kexiao, Chen Kedi, Chen Kezhong, Chen Kexin, Chen Keli, Chen Keyi, Chen Keqiang, Chen Keliang and others.

Chen Yanxi (1848-1929), the second son of Chen Gengyun, is the native of Chenjiagou Village, Wenxian County, Henan Province. He learned to practice Taijiquan from his father since he was young. He usually lay on the bench all night and practiced Taijiquan when he woke up. Besides the farming work, he taught his disciples skills. In the 26th year of Guangxu's reign (1900), Yuan Shikai came to Shandong as the governor and saw the monument set up for Chen Gengyun. Knowing that Chen family members were skilled in Taijiquan, he sent his followers to Wenxian County to invite Chen Gengyun to teach his sons and nephews Taijiquan. But Chen Gengyun had been dead for many years. So Chen Yanxi was invited to teach in Shandong. At that time, the other martial artists in Yuan's mansion were jealous of Yanxi at first and were only convinced by him after competing. Chen Yanxi accompanied Yuan from Shandong to Tianjin to teach Taijiquan and returned to his hometown due to his old mother after six years.

太极拳第八代代表性传承人和兆元画像

Portrait of He Zhaoyuan, One of the Representatives of the 8th Generation of Taijiquan Successors

太极拳第八代代表性传承人武禹襄画像
Portrait of Wu Yuxiang, One of the Representatives of the 8th generation of Taijiquan Successors

武禹襄（1812—1880），名河清，字禹襄，号廉泉，以字行世。清直隶广平府永年县（今河北省邯郸市永年区）人。廪贡生，以子侄贵赠封中宪大夫、兵部郎中加二级。自幼习练家传洪拳。初从杨露禅学陈氏太极拳老架。1854年至河南省温县师从陈清平学陈氏太极拳小架新创套路，月余始得精妙。后融会贯通，创造一套架式，自成一派，被称作武氏太极拳。武禹襄不以教拳为业，传人有二甥李亦畬、李启轩。李亦畬传郝为真，郝为真传孙禄堂。2008年6月14日，武氏太极拳入列第一批国家级非物质文化遗产扩展项目名录。

李景炎（1825—1893），又名李盾，河南省温县陈新庄人。初学于陈家沟拳师陈有伦，后拜陈清平为师，刻苦练拳。出师后，以保镖、授徒为业。晚年创编忽雷太极拳。李景炎传子李火焰及徒杨书文、张国栋。

李作智（1844—1914），字镜心，河南省温县南张羌村人。南张

He Zhaoyuan (1810-1890) was born into a traditional Chinese medicine family in Zhaobao Village, Wenxian County, Henan Province. He learned to practice Taijiquan painstakingly from Chen Qingping. Based on his years of practice and study, he developed a new style—He style Taijiquan by modifying the technique, footwork and posture of Chen style Taijiquan. He style Taijiquan focused on natural principle and law. He taught He style Taijiquan to his sons He Runzhi and He Jingzhi, his grandson He Qingxi and his disciple Miao Yansheng and others. On November 11, 2014, He style Taijiquan was listed in the first expansion group of national intangible cultural heritage.

Wu Yuxiang (1812-1880), also named Heqing, is from Yongnian County, Guangping Prefecture, Zhili Province in the Qing dynasty (Nowadays it belongs to Yongnian District, Handan City, Hebei Province). He was the scholar recommended by the local government and titled the grand master exemplar and the director of the Bureau of Military of War. Since he was young, he learned to practice Hong Boxing. Then he began to learn the Old Frame of Taijiquan from Yang Luchan. In 1854, he came to Wenxian County to learn the Small Frame of Taijiquan from Chen Qingping. Combining the different techniques, he created Wu style Taijiquan. Wu Yuxiang taught Taijiquan but not for a living. His disciples were his two nephews Li Yishe and Li Qixuan. Later, Li Yishe taught Taijiquan to Hao Weizhen, who taught Taijiquan to Sun Lutang. On June 14, 2008, Wu style Taijiquan was listed in the first expansion group of national intangible cultural heritage.

Li Jingyan (1825-1893), also named Li Dun, is from Chenxinzhuang Village, Wenxian County, Henan Province. He learned Taijiquan from Chen Youlun initially and later from Chen Qingping. He worked very hard in practicing Taijiquan. And after he learned well, he worked as a security guard and made his living by teaching students. In his later years, he created Hulei style Taijiquan. Li Jingyan taught Taijiquan to his son Li Huoyan and his disciples Yang Shuwen and Zhang Guodong.

Li Zuozhi (1844-1914), with the courtesy name Jingxin, is from Nangzhangqiang Village, Wenxian County, Henan Province. Nangzhangqiang Village was only four kilometers away from Zhaobao Town, so since he was young, Li Zuozhi learned from Chen Qingping in arts and martial arts, both of

羌村距赵堡镇仅4公里，李作智自幼师从陈清平习文练武，文武均得师传。晚年创编腾挪太极拳。李作智传李镐、周瑞祥、郭炳光、周勋、王明槐、赵振绪等。

王赐信（1815—1890），河南省河内县北冷村（今属河南省温县）人。师从陈清平学太极拳。晚年创编忽灵太极拳。王赐信传子王建中、王建都，侄王太平等。

任长春（1839—1910），河南省河内县西辛庄（今属河南省温县）人。在陈仲甡家做长工时随东家学练陈氏太极拳，后随陈清平学拳。晚年创编领落太极拳。其传人有子任应极和弟子杜元化等。

杨健侯（1839—1917），名鉴，杨露禅长子，自幼随父习拳，拳术刚柔并济，出神入化，刀、剑、杆各种器械无不精通。杨健侯接替父职在京授拳，秉性温和，宽厚仁慈，从不恃拳傲物，有极高武德。

杨班侯（1837—1892?），名钰，杨露禅次子，相貌清癯，富有臂力，自幼得父真传。有宿慧，多心得，善距踊，类猿猴，精太极大杆术，得其拳法之奥。咸丰年间，随父进京传拳。

李瑞东（1851—1917），名树勋，字文侯，号瑞东，别号烟霞逸士。清直隶武清县城东后街（今天津市武清区城关镇东街）人。光绪六年（1880）四月二十八日，瑞王府总管王兰亭接纳李瑞东为师弟，标志着李瑞东正式成为太极拳传人。李瑞东将所学所悟衍化生新，创李氏太极拳。2014年11月11日，李氏太极拳入列第一批国家级非物质文化遗产扩展项目名录。

太极拳第九代代表性传人主要有陈子明、傅振嵩、陈发科、陈省三、陈金鳌、陈克弟、陈克忠、全佑、杨澄甫、李经纶等。

陈子明（1878—1951），河南省温县陈家沟人。从小跟随父、叔学习太极拳，功夫纯厚，且备明拳理，年轻时已成名手。曾在怀庆府（今沁阳市）成立国术团体传授太极拳，从学者甚多。后经人推荐，到上海、南京、西安等地教练拳术。有《陈氏世传太极拳术》著作传世。

which were handed down by his teacher. In his later years, he created Tengnuo style Taijiquan. And his disciples are Li Gao, Zhou Ruixiang, Guo Bingguang, Zhou Xu, Wang Minghuai, Zhao Zhenxu and others.

Wang Cixin (1815-1890) is from Beileng Village, Henei County, Henan Province (Now it belongs to Wenxian County, Henan Province). He learned to practice Taijiquan from Chen Qingping. In his later years, he created Huling style Taijiquan. His disciples included his sons Wang Jianzhong and Wang Jiandu, his nephew Wang Taiping and others.

Ren Changchun (1839-1910) is from Xixinzhuang Village, Henei County, Henan Province (Now it belongs to Wenxian County, Henan Province). He learned to practice Taijiquan from his master Chen Zhongshen when he was hired as a labor worker in Chen's family. And then, he learned from Chen Qingping. In his later years, he created Lingluo style Taijiquan. His lineage holders were his son Ren Yingji and his disciple Du Yuanhua and others.

Yang Jianhou (1839-1917), also named Jian, is the eldest son of Yang Luchan. He learned to practice boxing from his father since he was young and his boxing skills were both rigid and flexible. He was proficient in different kinds of weapons such as knives, swords and sticks. Yang Jianhou took in his father's position to teach boxing in Beijing. Thanks to his generosity and kindness, he has improved martial ethics.

Yang Banhou (1837-1892), also named Yu, is the second son of Yang Luchan. He was handsome-looking and had strong arms. He learned to practice Taijiquan from his father since he was young. He was good at jumping and was proficient in Taiji rod techniques. In the reign of the Emperor Xianfeng, he came to Beijing to teach Taijiquan with his father.

Li Ruidong (1851-1917), also named Shuxun and nicknamed YanxiaYishi, is from Donghoujie Street, Wuqing County, Zhili Province (now it belongs to Dongjie Street, Wuqing District, Tianjin City). On April 28, 1880, Wang Lanting, the head of Prince Rui's mansion, accepted Li Ruidong as his junior fellow apprentice, which symbolized that Li formally became a lineage holder of Taijiquan. Li Ruidong integrated what he has learned and created Li style Taijiquan. On Nov.11, 2014, Li style Taijiquan was listed in the first batch of extended items of national intangible cultural heritage in China.

当时的南京国术馆馆长张之江、教务处朱国福、河南国术馆刘丕显、沧州武术名家姜容樵等人均为该书作序，赞其"抱负绝学而不倦于教诲""不私其家传之秘""立言不流于夸诞""使读者一目了然"。在陈子明南京授拳期间，结识了南京国术馆武术家、武术史研究家唐豪（字范生）。唐豪三赴陈家沟实地调查，查阅陈氏族谱、墓碑，走访遗老，掌握了大量史料，经反复考证，确认河南省温县陈家沟是太极拳发源地，陈王廷是太极拳创始人。

傅振嵩（1881—1953），号乾坤，河南省沁阳县人。著名武术教育家，太极拳家。早年于乡中习武，曾随陈延熙学陈氏太极拳，随陈铭标学忽雷太极拳，又学八卦掌等功夫，后出外继续学艺，功力日深。1928年应邀执教于南京中央国术馆，后又南下广州于两广国术馆任教，培养了大批太极拳及其他武术人才。他综合各家特点，自创傅氏太极拳、械套路，是近代武术史上的重要人物。

太极拳第九代代表性传承人陈发科照片

Chen Fake, One of the Representatives of the 9th generation of Taijiquan Successors

Major representatives of the 9th generation lineage holders of Taijiquan are Chen Ziming, Fu Zhensong, Chen Fake, Chen Xingsan, Chen jin'ao, Chen Kedi, Chen Kezhong, Quan You, Yang Chengfu and Li Jinglun.

Chen Ziming (1878-1951) is a native of Chenjiagou Village, Wenxian County, Henan Province. He learned to practice Tajiquan from his father and his uncle when he was young and became the master of Taijiquan because of his excellent skills and his rich knowledge of Taijiquan. He organized a martial arts groups to teach Taijiquan in Huaiqing Prefecture (now it is Qinyang City) and attracted many followers. Later, after being recommended, he taught Taijiquan in Shanghai, Nanjing, and Xi'an respectively. His work *The Art of Chen Style Taijiquan* was passed down and was prefaced by many famous people at that time such as Zhang Zhijiang, head of the Central Martial Arts School, Zhu Guofu, director of Teaching Affairs Office of the school, Liu Pixian of Henan Martial Arts School and Jiang Rongqiao, a famous martial artist from Cangzhou. They praised him as knowledgeable, selfless and generous in his teaching of Taijiquan. During his teaching of Taijiquan in Nanjing, Chen Ziming made acquaintance with Tang Hao (with the courtesy name Fansheng), a martial artist and researcher of martial arts from the Central Martial Arts School in Nanjing. Tang Hao has been to Chenjiagou Village to do research on Taijiquan on three occasions. After studying the genealogy and tombstones of the Chen Clan and interviewing the elders repeatedly, it was confirmed that Chenjiagou Village was the birthplace of Taijiquan and Chen Wangting, the founder of Taijiquan.

Fu Zhensong (1881-1953), with the pseudonym Qiankun, is from Qinyang County, Henan Province. He was a famous educator of martial arts and master of Taijiquan. He learned to practice boxing in the countryside in his early years. And later, he learned to practice Chen style Taijiquan from Chen Yanxi, Hulei style Taijiquan from Chen Mingbiao and the routines of Eight-diagram Palm and was skilled in martial arts due to his constant learning and practice. In 1928, he was invited to teach at the Central Martial Arts School in Naijing and the Liangguang Martial Arts School in Guangzhou. A large number of talents of Taijiquan and the other martial arts were cultivated. Combining the characteristics of various schools, he created Fu style Taijiquan and equipment routines and became an important figure in modern martial arts.

陈发科（1887—1957），字福生，河南省温县陈家沟人，陈长兴曾孙，师承其父陈延熙。曾任北京武术社社长。陈氏太极拳新架创编者。其从20世纪20年代末到50年代逝世，在北京授拳20余年，使陈氏太极拳走出陈家沟，为京城人士所识，被尊为"太极一人"。著名高徒有沈家桢、顾留馨、洪钧生、田秀臣、雷慕尼、李经梧、冯志强、肖庆林及其子照旭、照奎和女儿豫侠等。1963年，人民体育出版社出版《陈氏太极拳》一书，为其弟子沈家桢、顾留馨所著，其中一、二路太极拳（即新架）动作依据陈发科晚年拳照所定。

陈省三（1880—1942），河南省温县陈家沟人。自幼爱武喜文。先从太极拳名家陈延熙学拳15年，练成精湛技艺，后从陈鑫练拳习文。对太极拳大、小架皆精。他终生拳、理兼修，文武俱备。1939年9月，陈省三应邀到国民党第二战区副司令长官、前敌总指挥卫立煌部传授太极拳。后任教于温县师范及沁阳、修武、禹州等地，从其学拳者甚众。

陈金鳌（1899—1971），字文斗，河南省温县陈家沟人。生于太极世家，系陈垚嫡孙、陈鑫侄孙，囊获家学真传，并以继承发扬太极拳为己任。参订《陈氏太极拳图说》一书，1928年被河南大学聘请为武术教授，闻名遐迩。后因战乱，辗转各地，曾于汉口、宝鸡等地择徒授业。

陈克弟（1905—1984），河南省温县陈家沟人，陈氏太极拳第九代传人。幼年即偕堂弟克忠从族祖陈鑫学习太极拳械，得拳艺真谛。抗日战争爆发后旅居陕西西安，协助族兄金鳌教拳。20世纪50年代末，迁居河南开封，传授陈氏太极拳（小架）拳械。1976年，应开封市体委邀请，在开封市汴京公园设场传授陈氏太极拳（小架）拳艺，后又组织了多个陈氏太极拳辅导站点，随其练拳者达千余人之多。

陈克忠（1908—1966），字子纯，河南省温县陈家沟人。自幼随族祖陈鑫学习陈氏太极拳小架，拳艺精湛，理法独到，深得太极拳、械套路精髓。其师弥留之际，授以有关拳事文稿及《三三六拳谱》。20世纪40年代，流离在外谋生，解放后返回家乡，一边种田，一边授徒。先后

Chen Fake (1887-1957), with the courtesy name Fusheng, is a native of Chenjiagou Village, Wenxian County, Henan Province. He was the great-grandson of Chen Changxing and learned to practice Taijiquan from Chen Yanxi. He was the president of Beijing Martial Arts Association and the creator of the New Frame of Chen style Taijiquan. He has taught Taijiquan in Beijing for more than 20 years (from 1920s to 1950s), which helped Taijiquan known in Beijing. Therefore,Chen Fake was honored the top master of Taijiquan. His major disciples are Shen Jiazhen, Gu Liuxin, Hong Junsheng, Tian Xiuchen, Lei Muni, Li Jingwu, Feng Zhiqiang, Xiao Qinglin and his sons Chen Zhaoxu and Chen Zhaokui, and his daughter Chen Yuxia. In 1963, the book *Chen Style Taijiquan*, written by his disciples Shen Jiazhen and Gu Liuxin, was published at the People's Sports Publishing House. And the movements of Routine One and Routine Two (referred to as the New Frame collectively) were in accordance with the ones performed by Chen Fake on his pictures taken in his late years.

Chen Xingsan (1880-1942) is a native of Chenjiagou Village, Wenxian County, Henan Province. He loved martial arts and the arts as well when he was young. He initially learned Taijiquan from Chen Yanxi, a famous master of Taijiquan, for 15 years and learned the arts from Chen Xin. So, he was skilled in both the Big Frame and the Small Frame of Taijiquan and was proficient in the practice and theory of Taijiquan. In September 1939, he was invited to teach Taijiquan in the army led by Wei Lihuang, the deputy commander of the secend war zone and frontline commander-in-chief of Kuomintang goverment. Later, he taught Taijiquan in Wenxian Normal College and Qinyang, Xiuwu and Yuzhou with many followers.

Chen Jin'ao (1899-1971), with the courtesy name Wendou, is a native of Chenjiagou Village, Wenxian County, Henan Province. Born in a Taiji family and as Chen Yao's grandson and Chen Xin's grandnephew, he acquired the truth of Taijiquan and took it as his duty to develop and spread Taijiquan. He has participated in compiling *The Illustrated Canon of Chen Style Taijiquan* and was appointed as the professor of martial arts by Henan University in 1928. Later, because of the war, he has been to Hankou, Baoji and other places to teach Taijiquan.

Chen Kedi (1905-1984), a native of Chenjiagou Village and the 9th

授拳十余年，不收分文报酬，使太极拳小架在陈家沟再一次得以普及和提高。

全佑（1834—1920），字公甫，号保亭，清直隶大兴人，满族老姓吴福氏。杨露禅在京授拳时，与万春、凌山三人受益最佳，各得所长，全佑长于柔化。后全佑拜杨露禅次子杨班侯为师继续深造，兼得杨家父子之长。晚年根据自己的感悟对师传拳架逐步修订，后经子鉴泉修改定型，形成一套新的架式。鉴泉从汉姓吴，称吴鉴泉，人们便称这套架式为吴氏太极拳。全佑传人有子鉴泉，徒王茂斋、郭松亭、常远亭、夏公甫、齐阁臣等。2014年11月11日，吴氏太极拳入列第一批国家级非物质文化遗产扩展项目名录。

杨兆清（1883—1936），字澄甫，人称"三先生"，杨健侯子。幼承家学，勤奋钻研，寒暑苦练，功夫日深。杨澄甫将太极拳在其父健侯修订中架的基础上，再行修订，定型为杨氏太极拳大架，成为现在的杨氏太极拳。杨澄甫著有《太极拳术》《太极拳体用全书》。

李经纶（1832—1892），字亦畲，清直隶广平府城内西街人，武氏太极拳第二代传人，清代举人。22岁随母舅武禹襄学习太极拳，后放弃举业，苦心钻研、百般揣摩演练太极拳。一生以行医为业，终身致力于太极拳研究，著作有《五字诀》《撒放秘诀》《太极拳小序》《走架打手行功要言》等。

太极拳第十代代表性传人主要有陈照丕、陈照奎、郝和、王其和、洪均生、冯志强、顾留馨、陈伯先等。

generation lineage holder of Taijiquan, learned to practice Taijiquan and instruments from Chen Xin with his brother Chen Kezhong when he was young and gained the true essence of Taijiquan. After the outbreak of the War of Resistance Against Japan, he lived in Xi'an to help his brother Chen Jin'ao teach boxing. In the late 1950s, he moved to Kaifeng, Henan Province, to teach the Small Frame of Taijiquan. In 1976, at the invitation of the Sports Committee of Kaifeng City, he taught the Small Frame of Taijiquan in Bianjing Park, Kaifeng City and later organized several coaching stations with more than 1000 practitioners.

Chen Kezhong (1908-1966), with the courtesy name Zichun, is a native of Chenjiagou Village, Wenxian County, Henan Province. Since he was young, he learned to practice the Small Frame of Taijiquan from his ancestor Chen Xin and gained the true essence of Taijiquan and the instruments routines. He was awarded the manuscripts of Taijiquan and *Boxing 336* by Chen Xin. In 1940s, he became homeless and wandered from place to place. He returned to his hometown after the People's Republic of China was founded and began to teach Taijiquan without charging fees, which popularize the Small Frame of Taijiquan in Chenjiagou Village again.

Quan You (1834-1920), with the courtesy name Gongfu and the pseudonym Baoting, is a Manchu from Daxing, Zhili Province. He learned boxing from Yang Luchan in Beijing. At that time, Quan You, Wan Chun and Lingshan were the prominent disciples. Each of them had his strong points and Quan You was good at flexibility. Later, Quan You continued to learn from Yang Banhou, the second son of Yang Luchan. So he combined the advantages of both the father and the son of the Yang family. In his old years, he revised the boxing routines according to his understanding and these were finalized by his son Jian Quan to form a new style. Jian Quan shifted his family name to Wu in the Han people and was named Wu Jianquan. So the new style he formed was called Wu style Tajiquan. Quan You's successors included his son Jian Quan, and his disciples Wang Maozhai, Guo Songting, Chang Yuanting, Xia Gongfu, Qi Gechen and others. On November 11, 2014, Wu style Taijiquan was listed in the first expansion group of national intangible cultural heritage.

Yang Zhaoqing (1883-1936), with the courtesy name Chengfu, is the son

太极拳第十代代表性传承人陈照丕照片

Chen Zhaopi, One of the Representatives of the 10th generation of Taijiquan Successors

陈照丕（1893—1972），字绩甫，河南省温县陈家沟人。曾任全国国术国考评判委员、全国武术协会委员，被授予"全国太极拳名家"称号。学拳于叔祖陈延熙、陈鑫和三叔陈发科。1928年秋，北京同仁堂药店东家乐佑申、乐笃同兄弟托人聘太极拳师于陈家沟，族人公推其前往。1929年，应邀赴南京教拳，任中央国术馆名誉教授。1933年担任全国运动会国术裁判委员会委员和全国第二届国术国考评判委员会委员。1942年，受当时黄河水利委员会委员长张含英（解放后任水利部副部长）之邀，出任黄委会机关武术教官，直至中华人民共和国成立之后，陈照丕一直在黄委会工作。1958年退休回乡传拳。1962年，在全国武术大会上，被授予"太极拳名家"称号。著作有《太极拳入门》《陈氏太极拳汇宗》《太极拳引蒙》等。

郝和（1849—1920），字为真，河北永年人。从李亦畬学武氏太极拳，勤学苦练，功力日进。弟子孙禄堂创编孙氏太极拳。

王其和（1889—1936），字春山，河北省邢台市任县邢湾环水村人。师从郝为真学习武氏太极拳，师从杨澄甫学习杨氏太极拳，并受教

of Yang Jianhou. He learned to practice Taijiquan from his father and worked very hard. On the basis of the Middle Frame of Taijiquan revised by his father, he revised and finalized it as the Big Frame of Yang style Taijiquan, which is what Yang style Taijiquan is. He has written two books on Taijiquan as *Art of Taijiquan*, and *Essence and Applications of Taijiquan*.

Li Jinglun (1832-1892), with the courtesy name Yishe, one of the 2nd generation lineage holders of Wu style Taijiquan and a first-degree scholar in the Qing dynasty, is from Xijie Street, Guangping Prefectural City, Zhili Province. At the age of 22, he learned to practice Taijiquan from his uncle Wu Yuxiang and gave up his study to practice it. In his life, he was a doctor, but devoted all his efforts to Taijiquan study and wrote some passages, including *Song of Five Characters*, *Secrets on Releasing*, *Short Preface of Taijiquan* and *Essentials of Fighting*.

Major representatives of the 10th generation lineage holders of Taijiquan are Chen Zhaopi, Chen Zhaokui, Hao He, Wang Qihe, Hong Junsheng, Feng Zhiqiang, Gu Liuxin and Chen Boxian.

Chen Zhaopi (1893-1972), with the courtesy name Jifu, is a native of Chenjiagou Village, Wenxian County, Henan Province. He was a member of the National Wushu Examination and Judgement Committee and National Wushu Association, and was awarded the title of "National Taijiquan Master". He learned to practice Taijiquan from his grand uncles Chen Yanxi and Chen Xin and his uncle Chen Fake. In the autumn of 1928, Le Youshen and Le Dutong, who were the owners of Beijing Tongren Drugstore, decided to hire a boxer in Chenjiagou Village and he was recommended by his clan. In 1929, he was invited to teach Taijiquan in Nanjing and appointed as Honorary Professor of the Central Martial Arts School. In 1933, he was a member of the National Academic Judgement Committee of the National Games and the Second National Academic National Examination and Judgment Committee. In 1942, at the invitation of Zhang Hanying, then Chairman of the Yellow River Management Committee (Vice Minister of Water Resources since 1949), he served as *wushu* instructor of the Yellow River Management Committee. Since the founding of the People's Republic of China in 1949, he has been working there until he retired in 1958. Then he taught Taijiquan in his home place. In 1962, he was awarded the title

于孙禄堂。王其和晚年吸收多家拳种之精华创编了一套新架式，被后人称作王其和太极拳。2014年11月11日，王其和太极拳入列第一批国家级非物质文化遗产扩展项目名录。

洪均生（1907—1996），河南省禹县人，幼年时随父寓居京城，因体弱于1930年拜陈发科为师，学习陈氏太极拳15年不辍，深得陈发科真传。后困于家计，于1944年离京，辗转赴济南投亲谋生。1956年再度赴京，拜晤其师陈发科，以求拳法之精与拳理之密，更得陈发科晚年之技击精粹。征得陈发科同意，遂将师授之技法融于套路之中，为后学者开辟了一条掌握陈氏太极拳技击奥妙的捷径，后人称之为洪传陈氏太极拳。

顾留馨（1908—1990），上海市人，著名武术家。11岁开始习武，对杨氏和陈氏太极拳及推手有很深造诣。1959年受国家体委委托，赴河内任胡志明的太极拳教师。回国后应邀到中南海、北戴河和广州等地指导部分党和国家领导人练习太极拳。1956至1966年任上海体育宫主任，1979年任上海体育科研所副所长。1977年和1980年两次东渡日本讲学、授拳。1979年当选为中国武术协会委员和上海市武术协会主席，后应聘为上海体育学院兼职教授。主要著述有《简化太极拳》《太极拳术》《太极拳研究》《陈氏太极拳》《怎样练习简化太极拳》《炮捶》等。

陈伯先（1920—1989），字耀祖，号斌农，河南省温县陈家沟人。自幼随父陈以温习练太极拳。先后受教于陈子明、陈照旭、陈照丕等，更得陈克忠亲传，攻读了《陈氏太极拳图说》《三三六拳谱》等书，深得太极拳真谛。20世纪五六十年代，开设家庭武场，引导后生学拳，积极组织参加国内各类武术赛事。撰写《太极拳由来》《太极拳传递表》《忆三三六拳谱》等文章，编撰《陈氏太极拳练习概要》。历任省、市、县太极拳协会理事、副会长等职。

冯志强（1928—2012），河北省束鹿县（今辛集市）人。8岁开始练武，先后学练过少林桩拳、通臂拳、心意六合拳等，24岁时跟陈发科

of "Taijiquan Master" at the National Wushu Conference. His works included *Introduction to Taijiquan*, *On Chen Style Taijiquan* and *Guidance of Taijiquan*.

Hao He (1849-1920), with the courtesy name Weizhen, is from Yongnian, Hebei Province. He learned to practice Wu style Taijiquan from Li Yishe and worked diligently and made more progress. His disciple Sun Lutang created Sun style Taijiquan.

Wang Qihe (1889-1936), with the courtesy name Chunshan, is a native of Huanshui Village, Renxian County, Xingtai City, Hebei Province. He learned to practice Wu style Taijiquan from Hao Weizhen and Yang style Taijiquan from Yang Chengfu with the mentorship of Sun Lutang as well. In his later years, he absorbed the boxing essence of many schools and created a new style, which was called Wang Qihe Taijiquan. On November 11, 2014, Wang Qihe Taijiquan was listed in the first expansion group of national intangible cultural heritage.

Hong Junsheng (1907-1996), a native of Yuxian County, Henan Province, moved to live in Beijing with his father when he was young. Because of his poor health, he began to learn Taijiquan from Chen Fake in 1930. He was tutored in Chen style Taijiquan by Chen Fake for 15 years and gained its true essence. In 1944, under the pressure of life, he left Beijing to seek refuge with relatives in Jinan. In 1956, he returned to Beijing to visit his master, Chen Fake, to study the precise theories and methods of Taijiquan. There, he had acquired the essence of fighting from his masters. With the consent of Chen Fake, he integrated techniques taught by his master into the routines, developing a shortcut for the practitioners to learn the skills of Chen style Taijiquan, which was called Hong's Chen style Taijiquan.

Gu Liuxin (1908-1990), a Shanghai native and famous martial artist, learned to practice *wushu* at the age of 11. He has profound knowledge of Yang style Taijiquan, Chen style Taijiquan and pushing hands. In 1959, he was entrusted by China's National Sports Commission to teach Ho Chi Minh Taijiquan in Hanoi, Vietnam. After returning to China, he was invited to teach some state leaders Taijiquan in Zhongnanhai, Beidaihe and Guangzhou respectively. He was the director of Shanghai Sports Palace from 1956 to 1966 and the vice-director of Shanghai Sports Research Institute in 1979. He went to Japan to present lectures and teach Taijiquan in 1977 and in 1980 respectively. In 1979, he was

学习陈氏太极拳。1983年6月，北京市陈氏太极拳研究会成立，冯志强被推选为会长。为了普及陈氏太极拳，他结合多年教拳实践，取传统套路之精华，编创了《心意混元陈氏太极拳48式》，深受中外太极拳爱好者的喜爱。

太极拳第十一代代表性传人主要有孙禄堂、陈立清、陈立宪、陈庆州等。

太极拳第十一代代表性传人孙禄堂照片
Sun Lutang, One of the Representatives of the 11th Generation of Taijiquan Successors

孙禄堂（1860—1933），名福全，字禄堂，晚号涵斋，别号活猴，河北省完县人。幼学少林拳，1873年师从李魁元学习形意拳，两年后又随李魁元的师傅郭云深继续深造，后随程廷华学八卦拳。1912年，孙禄堂师从郝为真学习武氏太极拳。1918年，孙禄堂将形意、八卦、太极三家合冶一炉，参合三家之长，融会贯通，姿势参取杨氏，理论兼采形意，创造了架高步活的孙氏太极拳。

elected a member of National Wushu Association and Chairman of Shanghai Wushu Association. Later, he was appointed as a part-time professor of Shanghai Sports College. His main works include *Simplified Taijiquan, Taijiquan Skills, On Taijiquan, Chen Style Taijiquan, How to Practice Simplified Taijiquan and Boxing*.

Chen Boxian (1920-1989), with the courtesy name Yaozu, is a native of Chenjiagou Village, Wenxian County, Henan Province. When he was young, he learned to practice Taijiquan from his father Chen Yiwen. And later, he learned to practice Taijiquan from Chen Ziming, Chen Zhaoxu, Chen Zhaopi and Chen Kezhong respectively. He gained the essence of Taijiquan after reading *The Illustrated Canon of Chen Style Taijiquan* and *Boxing 336*. In the 1950s and 1960s, he set up a home school to teach Taijiquan and organized the students to participate in various martial arts competitions at national, provincial and regional levels. He has written some articles such as *The Origin of Taijiquan*, *The Lineage Chart of Taijiquan* and *In Memory of Boxing 336* and compiled *The Essentials on Practicing Chen Style Taijiquan*. He was a council member and vice-director of Taijiquan associations at different levels.

Feng Zhiqiang (1928-2012) is a native of Shulu County (now Xinji City), Hebei Province. At the age of 8, He began to practice *wushu* and successively learned Shaolin Zhuang Boxing, Arm Boxing and *Xinyiquan*. At the age of 24, he learned to practice Chen style Taijiquan from Chen Fake. He was elected the director of Chen style Taijiquan Research Association in Beijing in June, 1983. In order to popularize Chen style Taijiquan, on the basis of years of practice and teaching experience, he absorbed the essence of the traditional routines and compiled *48-Form Chen Style Hunyuan Taijiquan*, which is favored by the practitioners at home and abroad.

Major representatives of the 11th generation lineage holders of Taijiquan are Sun Lutang, Chen Liqing, Chen Lixian and Chen Qingzhou.

Sun Lutang (1860-1933), with the courtesy name Fuquan and nickname Monkey, was born in Wanxian County, Hebei Province. He learned to practice *Shaolinquan* in Childhood and *Xingyiquan* from Li Kuiyuan in 1873. And two years later, he continued to learn *Shaolinquan* from Guo Yunshen, Li Kuiyuan's master and then *Baguaquan* from Cheng Tinghua. In 1912, He learned to

太极拳第十一代代表性传人陈立清照片
Chen Liqing, One of the Representatives of the 11th Generation of Taijiquan Successors

　　陈立清（1919—2008），女，河南省温县陈家沟人。曾任陕西省西安市萃华武术馆馆长、名誉馆长，中国（温县）国际太极拳年会副秘书长、顾问。解放前夕迁居西安市，从事教育工作40余年，传拳60年。曾任西安市武协委员、陕西省武术挖掘小组成员，不断应邀参加各项武术比赛，被西宁市、长沙市、杭州市、沁阳市、平凉市等地武术组织聘为顾问。1975年，两次赴太原市和洪洞县许方庆处，觅回陈氏几近失传的"一百单八势太极长拳"。有《陈氏太极拳的风格》《学练太极拳十三要》《试用科学原理剖析太极拳的松、柔和技击》等论文发表，著有《陈氏太极拳小架》一书传世。

　　陈立宪（1923—1983），河南省温县陈家沟人，迁居沁阳市。深得祖传太极拳之奥妙。总结一生练拳经验，用现代科学翻译古老哲学，编成《陈氏太极拳拳式讲解》一书，整理出《陈氏太极拳练习要领》。利用解剖学、力学，从不同角度对太极拳理论进行验证，写下了数十万言的心得笔记。1965年，租赁房屋，自设教场，义招门徒。1976年之前倡办业余武术班。每日早上外出授拳，晚上在家精研拳理，还利用节假日

practice Wu style Taijiquan from Hao Weizhen. And in 1918, he combined the merits of *Xingyiquan*, *Baguaquan* and Taijiquan and created Sun style Taijiquan which featured with high posture and flexible footwork.

Chen Liqing (1919-2008), female, is a native of Chenjiagou Village, Wenxian County, Henan Province. She has been the curator and honorary curator of Cuihua Wushu School and the deputy secretary-general and consultant of the China (Wenxian) International Taijiquan Festival. She moved to Xi'an City before October 1949, and engaged in education for more than 40 years and teaching Taijiquan for 60 years. She has been a member of Xi'an Wushu Association and Shaanxi Wushu Developing Group. Being invited to participate in various martial arts competitions, she was hired as the consultant of martial arts organizations in Xining, Changsha, Hangzhou, Qinyang and Pingliang and so on. In 1975, she went to Taiyuan City and Hongdong County to visit Xu Fangqing twice to find the 108 postures of Taiji Changquan, which were nearly missing. She published many articles, including *On the Style of Chen Style Taijiquan*, *13 Essentials of Learning and Practicing Taijiquan*, *Analysis of Taijiquan's Looseness, Softness, and attack and defence by Using Scientific Principles*. And her book *The Small Frame of Taijiquan* has been handed down.

Chen Lixian (1923-1983), a native of Chenjiagou Village, Wenxian County, Henan Province, moved to Qinyang City. On the basis of his full understanding of the essence of Taijiquan and his whole life experience of practicing Taijiquan, he translated ancient philosophy with modern science and compiled *Explanation of Chen Style Taijiquan* and *Essentials of Practicing Chen Style Taijiquan*. By analyzing and verifying Taijiquan from anatomy and mechanics, he wrote notes with hundreds of thousands of words. In 1965, he rented a house to recruit his disciples for free. He advocated opening amateur martial arts classes before 1976. Every day, he went out to teach students Taijiquan in the morning and studied the theory and method of Taijiquan at home in the evening. And also he taught Taijiquan in other places on his holiday or his business trips. In 1983, he was honored as a National Excellent Wushu Instructor.

Chen Qingzhou (1934-2015) is a native of Xulv Village, Huangzhuang Town, Wenxian County, Henan Province. He has been the president of Qingzhou Wushu School in Wenxian County, the deputy secretary-general of China

和出差到外地教拳讲学。1983年，荣获"全国优秀武术辅导员"称号。

太极拳第十一代代表性传人陈庆州照片
Chen Qingzhou, One of the Representatives of the 11th Generation of Taijiquan Successors

陈庆州（1934—2015），河南省温县黄庄镇徐吕村人。曾任温县庆州武院院长，中国（温县）国际太极拳年会副秘书长，美国陈庆州功夫研究会太极拳总教练。1962年拜陈家沟陈照丕为师，潜心学艺，刻苦练功，精于"走化"。

(Wenxian) International Taijiquan Festival, and the coach of the Chenqingzhou Martial Arts Association in the United States. In 1962, he learned to practice Taijiquan from Chen Zhaopi and worked diligently and was good at dispersing force.

第二章

# 太极拳的理论体系

Chapter Ⅱ

The Theoretical System of Taijiquan

太极拳在整个运动过程中自始至终都贯穿着"阴阳"和"虚实",这在动作上表现为每个拳式都具有"开与合""圆与方""卷与放""虚与实""轻与沉""柔与刚"和"慢与快",并在动作中有左右、上下、里外、大小和进退等对立统一的独特形式。这是构成太极拳的基本原则。太极拳不仅在外形上,而且在内功上也有其特殊的要求。练习太极拳时,要求用意不用力;要求一动全动,节节贯串,连绵不断,一气呵成;要求有慢有快,快慢相间。它的力量,要求有柔有刚,刚柔相济;要求立身中正,虚中有实、实中有虚,开中寓合、合中寓开。具备了这些条件,太极拳才能充分发挥它的特殊作用。在体育保健上,太极拳不仅能增强运动器官与内脏器官的基本功能,并且能锻炼和增强意识的指挥和协调能力。太极拳在技击上也有独特作用:可以以轻制重,以慢制快,动作起来一动全动,"周身一家"。太极拳的理论体系主要有以下八个方面。

## 一、以心行气,以气运身,用意不用力

拳谱规定:以心行气,务令沉着,乃能收敛入骨;以气运身,务令顺遂,乃能便利从心;心为令,气为旗,气以直养而无害;全身意在神,不在气,在气则滞。

太极拳讲究用意练意、行气练气。在练拳时,要"以心行气":心为发令者,气为奉令而行的"传旗";一举一动均要用意不用力,先意动而后形动,这样才能做到"意到气到",气到劲到,动作才能沉着,久练之后气才能收敛入骨,达到"行气"最深入的功夫。

气受意的指挥,而这气并非一般所说的那种肺呼吸的空气,而是一种"内气"。这种气在中国传统医学理论中叫作"元气"或"正气",被认为是从母体中秉承下来的。在针灸和气功疗法中,至今仍沿用此说。武术家们则把这种气称为"内气""内劲"等,认为练到此气出现

The elements of "emptiness, fullness, yin and yang" are reflected so clearly in Taijiquan that each movement is expected to keep the balance between "openness and closeness", "roundness and square", "folding and stretching", "emptiness and fullness", "lightness and heaviness", "softness and hardness" and "quickness and slowness". Meanwhile the special feature of the unity of opposites is well demonstrated, such as the left and the right, the upper and the lower, the inside and the outside, the big and the small, and the forward and the backward. Taijiquan asks for strict requirements not only in terms of external positions, but also in terms of internal energy. In the practice of Taijiquan, focus should be put on intention rather than force; each part of the body is well coordinated with others, finishing every movement without any pause; the balance of slowness and quickness should be carefully kept in every movement. The energy involved in it should blend softness and hardness well. In the practice of Taijiquan, the practitioner should stand uprightly, and meanwhile he or she should keep a good balance between emptiness and fullness, openness and closeness. Only when those requirements are met, can Taijiquan show its special functions. In terms of sport health care, Taijiquan can not only strengthen the basic functions of locomotive and visceral organs, but also improve the command and coordination abilities of consciousness. In addition, Taijiquan also has special functions in the aspect of attack and defense. It can deal with strong force skillfully by small energy, and counteract fast strikes by slow ones. Moreover, once one part of the body moves, all the other parts will move together coordinately. The theoretical system of Taijiquan mainly includes the following eight points.

## I. Control *Qi* by Mind, Move the Body by *Qi*, and Focus on Intention Rather than Force

According to the Taijiquan classics, *qi* should be controlled by mind calmly and steadily so that it can be integrated with bones; the body should be moved by *qi* smoothly and naturally so that it can follow the heart harmoniously; the heart is like the order while *qi* the flag; the whole body should be centered on intention instead of *qi*; if the focus is put on *qi*, the body will be rigid and stiff.

Taijiquan values the concentration of intention and the control of *qi*. In practice, the heart should be focused to move *qi*. The heart is considered as the general who

并且能够掌握此气，功夫才算达到一定层次。

练太极拳最讲究"精神"，心意所发，气随意行，肢体运动一片活泼，精神自现；意境深邃，气敛于内，外现沉稳，一片虚灵；心态和平，意之所向，或进或退，或左或右，宜虚宜实，动荡转折，顺逆缠绕，无不圆转自如，得心应手。练太极拳先要使思想进入一种毫无杂念的状态，求得精神上的空灵境界，以便周身内外，从神经到五脏六腑、骨胳肌肤，都处于一种松静下的自我"感知"状态。如此，无论周身何处不顺遂，劲在何处犯顶，受力的作用及力的方向大小，都会及时被察觉并得到调整。在这种"意境"和"感知"状态下练拳，周身舒畅，练拳后会有如同沐浴过后的清爽感觉，就好像是大脑和五脏六腑都进行了一次清洗和净化，气清神明。

国家级非物质文化遗产项目太极拳代表性传承人——陈小旺
Chen Xiaowang, one of the Representative Inheritors of Taijiquan as the National Intangible Cultural Heritage

由于太极拳是意气运动，所以久练太极拳的人，只要思想上想到某一部位，就可以产生气的活动。因此，有不少人不惜岁月地早晚走架

gives the order, while *qi* is like soldiers that move after the order. In every movement, focus should be put on intention instead of the brute force. The body movement is always guided by intention and after a long time of practice, *qi* and force will be well coordinated with each other to improve the effect of *qi*'s movement.

*Qi* does not refer to the air that is breathed by the lung of the body, but a type of "inner *qi*", which is "the vital *qi*" or "the healthy *qi*" in traditional Chinese medicine. It is still widely used in the treatment of acupuncture and *qigong*. For martial artists, it is called "the inner *qi*" or "the inner force". Generally, after a long time of practice when one is able to sense *qi* and have a good command of it, he is said to have achieved a certain level of kung fu.

In the practice of Taijiquan, once *qi* is smoothly guided by the mind, the body movement will most probably be natural and flexible. At this moment, the practitioner will usually have a peaceful mind, ready to follow his heart to start various movements, backward or forward, left or right, upward or downward, stretching or spinning. Each part of the body, such as nerves, inner organs, bones, flesh and skin, has been able to reach a stage of relaxation and stillness. Therefore, if there is any physical awkwardness, the magnitude and direction of the force will be immediately perceived and adjusted. After practicing Taijiquan, the practitioner will definitely feel greatly refreshed as if he has just showered, or as if the brain and inner organs have been cleared and purified.

Since Taijiquan is a sport of intention and *qi*, those who practice it often will produce *qi*'s flow when thinking of one part of the body. Therefore, in order to reach this point, many practitioners are willing to take a lot of time in correcting their own frames of Taijiquan. Once the movement of the flesh and the internal organs are closely coordinated, *qi* and *jin* will be well guided by intention.

Like other martial arts featured by stillness, Taijiquan also attaches great value to the use of intention and *qi*'s flow. However, they are quite different. The former stresses the pure stillness, while the latter puts emphasis on the pursuit of stillness in movement. Since Taijiquan focuses on both internal and external practice and pursues stillness in movement, it has to show the vigorous self-possessed external air so as to improve the internal movement of intention and *qi*. As is stated in the work *Exposition of Insights into the Thirteen Postures*, "the practitioner of Taijiquan should look like an eagle that is about to attack a hare in terms of the form and act

子，并时时校正架子，正是为了做到这点。太极拳动作练成定型以后，大脑皮层中的兴奋和抑制过程就能准确地按一定程序交替活动；同时，肌肉也能协调地收缩与放松，即使偶然受到突然的刺激，也不会使这种协调的动作受到损害。做到这点，就表明肌肉的活动与内脏器官之间已建立了极巩固的协调关系，只要意到气就到，气到劲也到。

在用意气方面，太极拳和静功是相同的，都着重于练意与练气。但太极拳是在行动中练（动中求静），所以名之为意气运动；而静功则无行动，单独求静，因此两者不能混淆。正因为太极拳是内外俱练，动中求静，所以要做好内在的意气运动，就必须很好地显出外部的神气鼓荡。《行功心解》中说："形如搏兔之鹰，神似捕鼠之猫。"

实现太极拳意气运动的若干素质不是单独成立的，而是互为前提和基础，彼此之间相互依存、相互促进、相辅相成，并且相互制约，时时处处充满着矛盾与和谐。习练者正是要在这种充满矛盾与和谐的过程中，寻找最适合自己的平衡点，平衡四肢与躯干，平衡内外的气息，平衡自我与自然的关系。在一切平衡中，实现太极拳的意气运动。

## 二、身肢放长，周身弹性

拳谱规定：虚领顶劲，气沉丹田；含胸拔背，沉肩坠肘；松腰圆裆，开胯屈膝；神聚气敛，身手放长。

虚领顶劲和气沉丹田是身躯放长；含胸拔背是以前胸作支柱后背放长；沉肩坠肘是手臂放长；松腰圆裆和开胯屈膝，使腿部得以圆活旋转，是腿部放长的结果。所以太极拳的步法必须在圆裆松腰和开胯屈膝的姿势下用旋跟转腿来倒换虚实，外表看是腿的缠丝劲的表现，其实是内部促进了腿的放长。

这一系列放长，促成了全身放长，使身肢不但产生了弹性，形成掤劲，而且因全身放长，促使精神自然提振。因此，只要具备了放长的姿

like a cat that is ready to catch a rat in terms of the spirit".

The elements in Taijiquan are not separated from each other, but co-exist, restrict and promote mutually to each other. Any practitioner of Taijiquan has to understand the contradiction and harmony, and then produce good balance in different levels such as limbs and trunk, internal and external, and man and nature. When the balance is well kept, the Taijiquan movement will be guided well by intention and *qi*.

## II. Stretch Out the Body and Make Flexible Movements

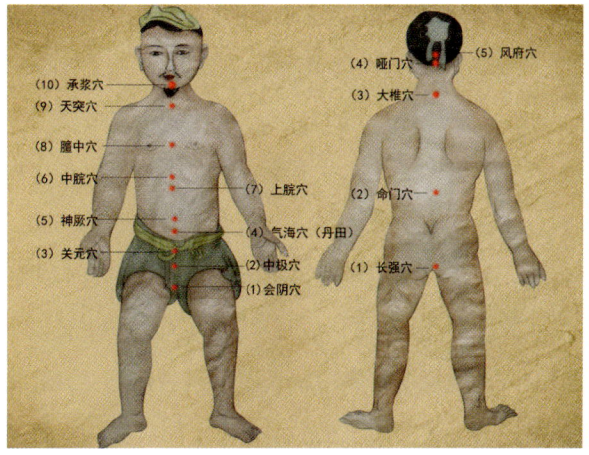

丹田穴位图

*Dantian* (No.4 on the left sketch) and Other Acupoints in a Human Body

According to the Taijiquan classics, in practice the practitioner should keep the head upright naturally, sink *qi* to *dantian*, contract the chest and broaden the back, lower the shoulders and elbows, relax the waist and arch the crotch, and stretch limbs and keep calm with a peaceful mind. In this way, every part of the body is able to be stretched out, including the head, the back, the arms and the legs. Therefore, the footwork methods of Taijiquan requires to spin heels and legs to shift emptiness and fullness when the practitioner relaxes waist, arches crotch and bends knees. It is the application of the silk-reeling *jin* to legs superficially, but it promotes the lengthening of legs actually.

势，就不易出现努责鼓劲（拙力）的毛病，为自然地松开和身手放长提供了条件。

## 三、螺旋的顺逆缠丝劲

陈鑫说，太极拳，缠法也。螺旋缠丝劲是陈氏太极拳的主要劲别特点。

太极拳必须运劲如缠丝。太极拳运劲的形象如同螺旋。这种螺旋必须走弧线，尤如子弹经过枪膛来复线的作用，运动于空间时，既有螺旋形的自身旋转，又有抛物线形的运动路线。太极拳的缠丝劲具有这种形象。

太极拳动作时，掌心由内往外翻或由外往内翻，使之形成太极图的形象。同时，由于掌心内外翻转，表现在上肢是旋腕转膀，表现在下肢则是旋踝转腿，表现在身躯则是旋腰转脊。三者结合起来，形成一条根在脚、主宰于腰而形于手指的空间旋转曲线。拳谱中特别提出，练拳时不论是开展的放开或紧凑的收敛，都不可须臾离开"翻转掌心"和"旋腕转膀"的太极劲。太极劲不是平面的一个圈，而是立体的螺旋上升。

螺旋的曲率半径是变化的，任何压力作用到这根螺旋杆上，都可因旋转落空而被化去。这是科学的化劲法。

太极拳技击的核心是"知己知彼"和"知机知势"的懂劲功夫。懂劲可分两个方面：一为自己懂劲，即懂得自己动作的劲，须从走架中得来；二为于人懂劲，即懂得别人的劲，须从推手中得来。欲求知人，必先知己，这是认识事物的过程。欲使走架子的"知己"达到高度纯熟的境界，则必须练成周身一家的功夫。周身一家的功夫是由内外相合和节节贯串中练成的，而这两者都产生于螺旋式的缠丝动作。因此在技击方面，缠丝劲也是极其重要的。

All the stretching movements not only make the body much more flexible and produce the force of warding off others, but they also make the mind more refreshed. Therefore, if the practitioner has stretched out his body, he will be most likely to avoid producing force rigidly and awkwardly.

## III. Start a Silk-Reeling *Jin*

According to Chen Xin, a late famous Taijiquan master, Taijiquan is actually the martial arts of reeling, and the silk-reeling *jin* is the most distinctive feature of Chen style Taijiquan. The spiral movement also needs to follow a trajectory, just as a bullet will not only turn on its axis spirally but also move in a trajectory when it runs out of a gun. The silk-reeling *jin* shows this movement feature very vividly.

In practice, the practitioner produces force just as if one is reeling silk in a spiral movement. The hand palms move in circles either from the inside to the outside, or from the outside to the inside, creating an image of the Taiji diagram. When the hand palms move, the wrists and the shoulders, the ankles and the legs, the waist and the backbone will move in circles accordingly. Those three parts of upper limbs, lower limbs and the middle body form a very coherent and coordinated movement curve. As mentioned in the Taijiquan classics, either outward stretching movement or inward contracting actions cannot separate from the silk-reeling jin of Taijiquan involved in rotating palms, wrist and shoulders. The curves in Taijiquan are not made horizontally, but made vertically with various upward changes.

When the radius of curvature of the spiral movement changes, any external force will be counteracted due to the rotation. It is the scientific method of counteracting force.

The core of attacking skills in Taijiquan lies in the ability of comprehending force, which mainly involves two aspects: firstly, comprehending one's own *jin,* which is acquired from the individual practice of the whole set of movements; secondly, comprehending another's *jin,* which is obtained through practice of pushing hands with others. It is a natural cognitive process that if one knows himself well one then understands others. If you want to have a very good command of your own *jin* in the individual practice, you must skillfully integrate the movements of each part of your body. The integration of movements mainly consists in the coordination of the inside

## 四、虚实转换得当

拳谱规定：意气须换得灵，乃有圆活之趣，所谓"变转虚实须留意"也；虚实宜分清楚，一处有一处虚实，处处总此一虚实；立身须中正安舒，支撑八面；上下相随人难侵；尾闾正中神贯顶，上下一条线。

太极拳所有动作必须分清虚实。动作能够虚实转换，就可耐久不疲。练太极拳时，双手要有虚实，双足也要有虚实，尤其重要的是，左手和左足、右手和右足要上下相随、分清虚实，也就是说，左手实则左足虚，右手虚则右足实。这是调节内劲使之保持中正的中心环节。此外，形成落点的虚中要有实，实中要有虚，从而做到处处总有虚实，使内劲处处达到中正不偏。初学时，动作大虚大实，以后逐步做到小虚小实，最后达到内有虚实而外面不见有虚实的境界，这是调整虚实的最深功夫。

虚实灵换的核心，在于意气的灵换，同时要在"中土不离位"及内劲中正的情况下来完成，因此，练拳时必须做到"尾闾正中""安舒支撑八面""虚领顶劲""上下一条线"地随时调整虚实。

## 五、节节贯串

拳谱规定：腰脊为第一主宰，一动无有不动；周身节节贯串，毋使丝毫间断；欲要周身一家，先要周身无有缺陷；行气如九曲珠，无微不到。

and outside of the body, as well as the coherent transition of one movement after another. Generally both aspects come from the silk-reeling jin. Therefore, the silk-reeling *jin* is very essential to developing attacking skills.

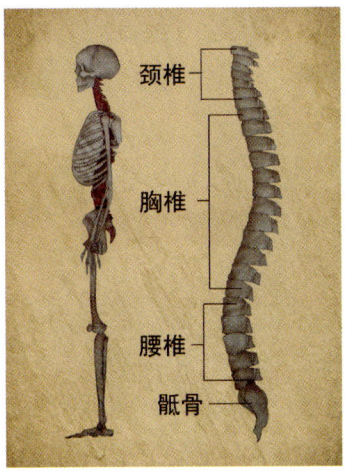

尾闾示意图
A Diagram of the Spine of a Human Body

# IV. Shift Emptiness and Fullness Appropriately

According to the Taijiquan classics, an appropriate shift of emptiness and fullness largely depends on the alteration of the mind and *qi*. Besides, emptiness and fullness, which coexist in every movement, should be distinguished from each other. Generally, the trunk of the body should be kept upright and relaxed to coordinate with the movements of the limbs. The upper will coordinate with the lower, the left with the right so that others cannot easily strike you.

Actually, emptiness and fullness should be clearly distinguished from each other in all the movements, which may make you feel refreshed instead of exhausted. In practice, the left hand should be coordinated with the left leg. If the left hand focuses on emptiness, then the left leg should focus on fullness. It is also true for the right hand and right leg. It is the key point to adjust the inner force and keep the body upright. In addition, for every point on your body, there should involve both emptiness and fullness, whether the former or the latter is the dominating factor. Only if the two sides supplement and coordinate with each other, may the inner

国家级非物质文化遗产项目太极拳代表性传承人——王西安
Wang Xi'an, One of the Representative Inheritors of Taijiquan as the National Intangible Cultural Heritage

太极拳动作要一动全动。腰是左右平行转动的中轴，脊是上下弯曲的根基。为达到一动全动，必须以腰脊为中心，在运动线路上不能单纯地左右平旋，也不能在上下、前后做弯曲动作，而必须将腰脊联合起来，使运动的路线形成一条既是左右，又是上下、前后的空间曲线，以建立一动全动的基础。这就是说，只有通过腰脊为中心，才可以使身体主要的运动关节依次动起来。此外，还要做到周身无缺陷，贯串如九曲圆珠，这样功夫才可以进展到周身一家的地步。

## 六、一气呵成

拳谱规定：往复须有折迭，进退须有转换；收即是放，放即是收；劲断意不断，意断神可接；如长江大河，滔滔不绝，一气呵成。

太极拳不以一动全动为满足，而是要求做到一气呵成，内劲不断，

force be produced smoothly and properly. For beginners, the movement may usually put too much stress either on emptiness or on fullness. However, gradually they will learn to keep the balance between the two, and finally they will achieve the ideal realm of martial arts, in which emptiness and fullness can only be felt within the body while others will not see anything awkward from the outside. This is the biggest requirement for the flexible adjustment of emptiness and fullness.

The shift of emptiness and fullness centers on the shift of intention and *qi*, and meanwhile it should be finished when the practitioner keeps the body balanced and controls the internal *jin* well. In a word, in the Taijiquan practice, a practitioner should keep the spine in the right central place, adopt a safe and coordinated posture to support the whole body, keep the head upright naturally and maintain the upper and the lower parts of the body in the same line coordinately.

## V. Coordinate Every Part of the Body

According to the Taijiquan classics, as the essential part of the human body, the waist and the spine will never keep still during the physical exercise; each part of the body is well-coordinated with others; the various parts of the body are integrated into one, and no awkward transition and cooperation will be found; *qi* should be delivered to all the likely places.

In the practice of Taijiquan, if one part of the body begins to move, the other parts of the body should move accordingly. The waist is the central axle around which the body can turn horizontally. The spine is the basis for which the body can fold or bend down vertically. To involve all the parts of the body into the movement, the waist and the spine must be taken as the center, either the simple horizontal turning movement or the pure vertical bending action is not required, and the movement should be complicatedly integrated, involving the leftward, the rightward, the upward, the downward, the forward and the backward. That is to say, only by taking the waist and spine as the center, the major joints can begin to move one by one. In addition, a practitioner should take every act smoothly like moving round beads, without showing any physical awkwardness in every part of the body. Only by achieving this, can he or she reach a stage in which the different parts of body are integrated into one.

这是加大运动量的又一方法。其具体方法是：在手法上遇到往复时，要嵌进折叠；在步法上遇到进退时，要嵌以转换；在开合、收放时，要有收即是放和放即是收的意和劲。当然，这个特点同第五方面叙述的特点一样，是在螺旋式缠丝运动的辅助下实现的。如果在发劲之后出现了断劲现象，就要将这种发劲的余意接续下去。万一意也断了，则要运用意、劲的余神接续下去。为了做到这点，劲要有折叠转换，动作要用意不用力，使收放统一的身法如同长江水流滔滔不绝，中间无卸劲的余地，亦无意驰的时候，这样就自然可以达到一气呵成的要求。

## 七、刚柔相济

拳谱规定："运劲如百炼钢，何坚不摧"；"极柔软，然后极坚刚"；"外操柔软，内含坚刚，而求柔软之于外，久而久之，自得内坚刚；非有心之坚刚，实有心之柔软也"；"太极拳决不可失之绵软。周身往复，以精神意气为本，用久自然贯通焉"；"运劲之功夫，先化硬为柔，然后练柔成刚。及其至也，亦柔亦刚。刚柔得中，方见阴阳。故此拳不可以刚名，亦不可以柔名，直以太极之无名名之"。

太极拳的学习，首先要摧毁人们动作中原有的坚硬劲，使它化为柔软，这是化柔的时期。这个时期愈长，则愈可把僵硬摧毁得彻底。这一时期的要点，是仍要不失绵软，在柔软之下，向着更有弹性的坚刚上迈进。这个刚，不是通过努责和鼓劲而产生的"生铁"的刚，而是由松开和放长而产生的弹性的刚。因为身肢放长，并不断螺旋式地绞来绞去，就可产生这种弹性，因此，又可名为"掤劲刚"。只有这种具有弹性的刚，才能达到"外操柔软，内含坚刚"的要求。这种刚柔的变换是由精神意气的隐显来掌握的。功夫精进后，劲可内隐得极深，使外形显得极柔，使人感到好像又回复到柔上去了，其实内在的质量却更加刚了。要达到刚柔相济的要求，必须依次经历求软摧僵、练柔成刚、刚柔变换、

## VI. Move Smoothly Without Pause

According to the Taijiquan classics, there should be a smooth transition between any two connected movements; the end of the previous movement is the beginning of the next one; the force is seemingly over at the end of one movement while the mind actually keeps going on to the other all the time; the whole set of movements is like an incessant river running vigorously.

To put it simply, in the practice of Taijiquan, the practitioner should make no pause in the movements, provide no chance to release the force, and spare no time to loosen the mind, thus finishing the whole set of movements naturally and smoothly.

## VII. Keep the Balance between Hardness and Softness

According to the Taijiquan classics, the practice of Taijiquan is just like making steel; as highly repeated smelting will produce high quality steel, consequently the frequent practice of Taijiquan will bring out firm force. The exterior will usually display softness while the interior often contains hardness. To get a good command of force, the practitioner will first learn to be gentle in movement and then gradually manage to turn softness into hardness. For great Taijiquan masters, hardness and softness are perfectly blended into each other and therefore a good balance between yin and yang can be maintained.

In other words, in practice of Taijiquan, the practitioner should turn the stiffness into softness first. The longer the process lasts, the more stiffness will be reduced. The key point at this stage is that the practitioner should put the focus on softness, and at the same time add some flexible hardness to the movements. Here hardness does not mean the awkward stiffness, but results from the relaxed movements of the extended body. Gradually, softness and hardness can be transformed so naturally and smoothly that the exterior looks very gentle while the interior is actually full of the force. Briefly speaking, to reach the perfect balance between hardness and softness, one should experience four stages, namely, seeking softness and avoiding stiffness, turning softness into hardness, transforming between hardness and softness, and reaching a good balance between the two sides.

刚柔相济四个过程。

## 八、快慢相间

拳谱规定：动急则急应，动缓则缓随；彼不动，己不动，彼微动，己先动；初学宜慢，慢不可痴呆，习而后快，快不可错乱；形抗五岳，势压三峰，由徐入疾，由浅入深。

初练太极拳套路时，动作应该越慢越好，可将时间放长，动作放慢，这样才有修改的机会，才能检查出不顺遂的地方。但是，慢不可慢到面部表现痴呆，这是慢的限度。以后，随着熟练程度的提高，可渐渐加快，缩短走一趟架子所需的时间。但由慢转快，同样也要有一个限度，要做到虽快但动作仍能沉着，仍能表现劲别，并不至于发生浮飘与错乱的现象。在能慢能快的总前提下，用到每个拳式时则须将这种快慢的对立面统一。每一个拳式到转关处要慢，过了转关处就逐渐加快，运到落点时最快，以后复转慢，如此周而复始。所以太极拳的每个拳式都要经过能慢能快的锻炼，这样才能在推手时"彼微动，己先动"，"动急则急应，动缓则缓随"，创造有利于自己的条件，并能达到快慢相间的统一。

## VIII.　Alternate with Quickness and Slowness

According to the Taijiquan classics, one will not move if the other keeps still; one will move first if the other begins to move. Beginners should learn to make slow movements, but never stagnant ones, and then gradually make quick ones, but never in disorder. They should keep an upright posture, show powerful manners, and learn gradually from slow into fast, from easier to harder.

To put it in another way, for beginners, the slower the movement, the better the results will be. Once the actions slow down, one may grasp every opportunity to feel the clumsiness and correct it. However, the movement should not be too slow, or else the practitioner will easily put on a silly facial expression and produce rigid movements. Gradually, the speed of the movement can be increased little by little, but not too quick. In other words, the movement should be started calmly, steadily and orderly. Besides, one should know when to slow down and when to speed up, and as a result he will be able to take a good command of the proper rhythm to reach the balance of slowness and quickness.

# 第三章
# 太极拳的技术体系

## Chapter III

## The Technical System of Taijiquan

太极拳的技术体系主要是太极十三势。太极十三势即太极拳五步八法，包括进、退、顾、盼、定五种步法和掤、捋、挤、按、採、挒、肘、靠八种技击法，其中分别包含粘、连、黏、随、不丢顶劲五种阴劲和掤、捋、挤、按、採、挒、肘、靠八种阳劲。

粘连黏随，即不丢不顶之劲，主进退，为太极推手中最需要之基本内劲。掤、捋、挤、按、採、挒、肘、靠等八法，可以用姿势表现出来，可以称作阳劲。粘、连、黏、随，没有固定姿势可以标榜，可以称作阴劲。

# 一、太极拳的五种步法和太极五步劲别

太极五步是太极十三势中的五种步法，即进、退、顾、盼、定。这五种步法暗含太极拳的五种劲别，即粘、连、黏、随和不丢顶劲，同时也对应人体经络脏腑的有关窍位，并与金木水火土五行对应。

太极拳的五种步法：

1. 前进：在五行中属水，方位正北。人体对应穴位是会阴穴，此穴属肾经。此劲的劲源在会阴穴，如欲前进，只要意在会阴穴，眼神向前上方看，身体即自然前进。从外表看，此劲只表现在步法上。蕴于内者，即粘劲。

2. 后退：在五行中属火，火能化万物，方位正南。人体对应穴位为印堂穴，此穴属心经。劲源在印堂穴，如欲后退，只要意想印堂穴，眼神向前下看，身体便会自然后退。从外形上看，此劲只表现在步法上。蕴于内者，即连劲。

3. 左顾：在五行中属木，木属直性，方位正东。人体对应穴位为

The technical system of Taijiquan lies mainly in the thirteen postures of Taijiquan. The thirteen postures of Taijiquan are the five footwork methods(Advancing, Retreating, Looking left, Gazing right and Central equilibrium) and eight techniques of Taijiquan (Warding off, Rolling back, Pressing, Pushing, Pulling down, Splitting, Elbowing and Shouldering). There are five types of *yin jin*: adhering, connecting, sticking following, and the *jin* of no releasing and resisting. There are also eight types of *yang jin*: Warding off, Rolling back, Pressing, Pushing, Pulling down, Splitting, Elbowing and Shouldering.

Adhering, connecting, sticking and following are the *jin* of no releasing and resisting. They dominate advancing and retreating, constituting the essential *jin* in pushing hands. The eight techniques of Taijiquan, namely, Warding off, Rolling back, Pressing, Pushing, Pulling down, Splitting, Elbowing and Shouldering, can be called *yang jin* because they can be demonstrated by postures, while adhering, connecting, sticking and following, which are not confined to fixed postures, can be called *yin jin*.

# Ⅰ. The Five Footwork Methods and Their Corresponding Types of *Jin* of Taijiquan

The five footwork methods of Taijiquan are Advancing, Retreating, Looking left, Gazing right and Central equilibrium of the thirteen postures of Taijiquan. They are accompanied by five kinds of *jin* of Taijiquan: adhering, connecting, sticking, following, and the *jin* of neither releasing nor resisting. They also correspond to the relevant acupoints of the human body's meridians and organs, and to the Five Elements (metal, wood, water, fire, earth) as well.

The Five Footwork Methods of Taijiquan

1. Advancing. According to the theory of the Five Elements, it belongs to water and lies in the due north. Its corresponding acupoint in the human body is the *huiyin*, which is called the kidney meridian. The source of this *jin* is in the *huiyin*. If you want to advance, as long as your intention is in the *huiyin* and you look upward, your body will advance naturally. Outwardly, this *jin* is expressed only in footwork. What is contained inside is the *jin* of adhering.

2. Retreating. According to the theory of the Five Elements, it belongs to

夹脊穴，此穴属肝经。此劲的劲源在夹脊，如欲侧转前进，只要意想夹脊穴往实脚之涌泉穴上落，身体便会自然地侧旋着前进。从外形上看，表现在步法上。蕴于内者，即黏劲。

4. 右盼：在五行中属金，方位正西。人体对应穴位是膻中穴，此穴属肺经。此劲的劲源在膻中穴。如欲侧转后退，只要右手抬至与乳平（即以拇指与膻中穴相平），同时左手抬起至肚脐与心窝之间，而左右两手心均向下，意想膻中穴微收，眼神顺左手食指往下看，身体便会自然地侧转后退。上述为左虚右实，反之亦然。从外表看，表现在步法上。蕴于内者，即随劲。

国家级非物质文化遗产项目太极拳代表性传承人——朱天才
Zhu Tiancai, One of the Representative Inheritors of Taijiquan as the National Intangible Cultural Heritage

fire and lies in the due south as fire can transform everything. Its corresponding acupoint in the human body is the *yintang*, which is called the heart meridian. The source of this *jin* is in the *yintang*. If you want to retreat, as long as your intention is in the *yintang* and you look downward, your body will retreat naturally. Outwardly, this *jin* is expressed only in footwork. What is contained inside is the *jin* of connecting.

3. Looking left. According to the theory of the Five Elements, it belongs to wood and lies in the due east as wood is straightforward. Its corresponding acupoint in the human body is the *jiaji*, which is called the liver meridian. The source of this *jin* is in the *jiaji*. If you want to move sideways and advance, as long as your intention is to fall the *jiaji* on the *yongquan* of the foot with the full step, your body will move sideways and advance naturally. Outwardly, this *jin* is expressed only in footwork. What is contained inside is the *jin* of sticking.

4. Gazing right. According to the theory of the Five Elements, it belongs to metal and lies in the due west. Its corresponding acupoint in the human body is the *danzhong*, which is called the lung meridian. The source of this *jin* is in the *danzhong*. If you want to move sideways and retreat, as long as the right hand is raised to the level of the *danzhong*, and the left hand is raised to the navel and the heart pit, with both the left and right hands facing downward; while you look down following the left index finger, your body will naturally turn sideways and retreat. Here your left step is empty and your right step is full, and vice versa. Outwardly, this *jin* is expressed only in footwork. What is contained inside is the *jin* of following.

5. Central equilibrium. According to the theory of the Five Elements, it belongs to earth and lies in the center. Its corresponding acupoint in the human body is the *dantian*, which is called the spleen meridian. The source of this *jin* is in the *dantian*. If you want to build a stable center of gravity, as long as your intention is in the *mingmen* and the navel, you will be as stable as a mountain. Therefore, the five stepping methods correspond to the Five Elements, and the Five Elements correspond to the five sense organs in the human body. Outwardly, it is reflected in footwork. What is contained inside is the *jin* of no releasing and resisting.

5. 中定：在五行中属土，方位正中央。人体对应穴位是丹田穴，此穴属脾经。劲源在丹田，如欲立稳重心，只要意想命门和肚脐，立刻会身稳如山岳。所以说五步对应五行，五行在人体中又对应五穴。从外表看，表现在步法上。蕴于内者，即不丢顶劲也。

太极五步劲别：

1. 粘劲：主前进。粘劲带有主动性，系用自己的手、腕、臂来粘对方的手、腕、臂，将对方粘起，使对方引进落空，达到牵动四两拨千斤的目的，为太极拳推手中最重要之基本内劲。粘劲要求轻灵，周身放松，手上绝对不可用力。

2. 连劲：即连贯也。连绵不断，不脱离，无停无止，无声无息。太极推手，实应有进有退，有化有发，退如得势，则发亦自随矣。其上身看似往后退，而意气已前进矣，此为以退作进之法。进则要有粘，退则要有连，诚奥妙无穷焉。反之，初学者在对方用力推来时，没有连劲，身体单纯后退，形成兵败如山倒之势，被迫跌出，乃不懂连劲也。真正懂连劲之后，即能得屈、伸、动、静之妙，开、合、升、降之效。见进则退，遇出则合，看来则让，就去即升。果能到此地步，即人懂劲境界也。

3. 黏劲：如粘如贴，不丢不顶，彼进我退，彼退我进，彼浮我随，彼沉我松，丢之不开，投之不脱，黏劲在太极推手中可化解掤、挤、按等进攻手法。当对方进攻时，我周身放松，特别要放松自己的手和臂，不与来力抗拒。否则手用力反抗，即暴露了腰部劲源，反抗之手或臂即成为自己之劲端，易被对方通过劲端，击中劲源。应在对方来力未接触自己身体之前，即全身放松，立即意念夹脊穴，对准来力接触我之部位，轻轻黏住往侧面移动，使对方发力落空。注意黏劲在对方来力落空未跌出前，不可离开。

4. 随劲：随即顺从、跟随之意，缓急相随，不即不离，进退相

*Jin* in the Five Footwork Methods of Taijiquan

1. Adhering. It dominates advancing. It takes the initiative to adhere to the opponent's hands, wrists and arms with one's own hands, wrists and arms. It adheres to each other together and leads the opponent into emptiness, so as to deflect a thousand pounds with four ounces. It is the most important basic internal *jin* in pushing hands of Taijiquan. Adhering requires an agile and relaxed body with no strength from hands.

2. Connecting. It means coherence and continuity with no separation. In Taijiquan pushing hands, there are both advancing and retreating, and both dispersing and issuing. If one gains advantages in retreating, then issuing force will follow. The upper part of the body looks like it is retreating, intention and *qi* have already advanced. This is the way of retreating in order to advance. Advancing requires adhering while retreating, connecting. How wonderful! On the contrary, when being pushed hard by the opponent, if you are a beginner of Taijiquan, you may simply retreat and are forced to fall back. This indicates that you do not know how to connect. If you really understand connecting, you can obtain the benefits of bending, extending, motion and stillness as well as opening, closing, ascending and descending. If you see the opponent advancing, you can retreat and unite. When the attack comes, you can yield. When the attack is gone, you can attack. This is the stage of comprehending *jin*.

3. Sticking. If you stick to the opponent, you will not release or resist. If your opponent advances, you can retreat, and vice versa. If your opponent moves lightly, you can follow. If your opponent moves heavily, you can relax. Sticking can dissolve some offensive tactics including warding off, pressing and pushing in pushing hands. When the opponent attacks, you should relax your entire body, especially your hands and arms, and do not resist the incoming force. Otherwise, if you resist vigorously with your hands, it will expose the *jin* source on the waist. And the hand or arm of resistance becomes an end of *jin,* through which the *jin* source is easy to be hit by the opponent. You should relax the whole body before the incoming force, and immediately concentrate your intention on the *jiaji* acupoint. By aiming at the position where the incoming force touches you, you gently stick and move aside, so that force is lost. You should notice that your sticking can not stop until the incoming force from the other party is lost.

依，不先不后，舍己从人。对方主动我为被动，随其后而行。所谓亦步亦趋也。太极拳有舍己从人之术，对方接触自己身体何处，该处即应相随而灵活。假使接触手，手不单要放松还要保持灵活；接触肘，肘放松仍要灵活；接触胸部，胸要放松灵活，周身处处都应如此。

  5. 不丢顶劲：要练于内，形于外，只有内外合一才能灵活奏效。中定不离位，含胸把腰松。对方来势，或高或低，或横或直，或左或右，或长或短，不能肯定。或先得能定步走化，当走化对方来力，意念要集中在丹田，前方来力，意想肚脐贴命门；后方来力，意想命门贴肚脐。不要与之相抗，当松开其来力后，劲源反之则为发，必使对方弹跳跌出。手或臂一觉着力，随即放松变为虚，如遇偏重则松之，遇双重则偏沉之，随彼之来力方向而去，卸去其力，不稍抵抗，使人处处落空，毫不得力，所谓左重则左虚，右重则右杳。意念守住丹田，变化在肚脐命门之间，全身松静，保持我顺人背，若能达此境界，对方虽有千斤之力，亦无法施用。轻灵玄妙，能收四两拨千斤之效。

  粘连黏随之劲，由推手而来。初练时两手不知所觉，犹如木棍；逐渐由手而臂、而胸、而背，乃至周身皮肤，逐渐生有感觉，有感觉如可粘黏，有粘黏始可将敌吸住，为我所制。故练习此劲至相当程度后，皮肤上有似云似雾之气，如漆似胶。一逢对手，即不丢不离。非但两手如此，周身皆然。其技艺愈高，气愈厚，且面积愈大。

## 二、太极拳的八门劲别和太极八法

  太极拳要求用意不用力，"力"指拙力，不指劲。太极拳有八门劲，八门劲均具有放长的弹性。

  八门劲别分别是：

  1. 掤劲：在全动之下掌心由内向外缠丝，称为掤劲；

4. Following. It means to go along with or to follow. Quickness and slowness follow each other. Advancing and retreating follow each other. When the other side takes the initiative, you are passive and move by following the other side. It is so called step by step. Taijiquan has the skill of giving up one's own to follow the other. The position where the other party touches you should be agile. If the hand is touched by the other side, it should not only be relaxed but also remain agile; if the elbow is touched, it should still be relaxed but agile; if the chest is touched, it should be relaxed and agile; it is the same case with other body parts.

5. No releasing and resisting. You should practice pushing hands internally and externally. Only unity of the internal and the external can lead to flexibility and effectiveness. The central equilibrium must be fixed and you should relax your waist when contracting the chest. You are uncertain that the attack from the other side is either high or low, straight or horizontal, left or right, and long or short. It is likely to have fixed steps to disperse the incoming force at first. At this time, you should concentrate on the *dantian*. If the force is coming from the front, you should have the intention of sticking the navel to the *mingmen*. If the force is coming from the back, you should have the intention of sticking the *mingmen* to the navel. Do not fight against the incoming force. When you disperse it, there will be issuing from source of *jin*, and the other party will be bounced off. When you feel the force of your hand or arm, it relaxes and becomes empty. When the left feels weight, then the left becomes empty. When the right feels weight, then the right is gone. The intention is on the *dantian*, and it moves between the navel and the *mingmen*. You should keep relaxed and still to follow the other. At this stage, even if the other has one thousand pounds of strength, four ounces can deflect that if your body is light and agile.

Adhering, connecting, sticking and following come from pushing hands. When practicing at first, the hands are not sensitive to the different type of *jin*; gradually the *jin* of adhering and sticking can be felt by the hands, then to arms, chest, back, and even the skin of the whole body. Adhering and sticking can help you to dominate the opponent. Therefore, after practicing for some time, a skilled practitioner will have gluing *qi* around his skin and will not release or resist when he is confronted with an opponent. Such is the case with the two hands and the whole body at large. The more skilled one is, the thicker the *qi* is, and the larger its

2. 捋劲：在全动之下掌心由外向内缠丝，称为捋劲；

3. 挤劲：双手同时将掤劲交叉向外发出，称为挤劲；

4. 按劲：掌心向下圈沾着一点而不离开的下掤劲，称为按劲；

5. 採劲：两手交叉向左右平，前后双分的掤劲，称为採劲；

6. 挒劲：将掤劲卷蓄起来，短距离内猛然抖弹而出，称为挒劲；

7. 肘劲：手腕出了方圆圈，将肘的掤劲发出去，称为肘劲；

8. 靠劲：肘出了方圆圈，将身躯的掤劲发出去，称为靠劲。

八门劲别中，掤劲是最基本的劲。

太极八法：

太极八法，指的是太极拳技击中的掤、捋、挤、按、採、挒、肘、靠八种基本手法和劲别，分别与八卦和八方一一对应。其中，掤、捋、挤、按为正法，称四正法或四正手，简称四正；採、挒、肘、靠为奇法，称四隅法或四隅手，简称四隅。八法以掤为首，四正为主，四隅为辅。

1. 掤：太极拳技击中，向上向外之力为掤，用于化解或合力发人。

双方搭手，对方进身做攻势，以手前进，我则逆敌方向，以向上向外劲力承应，使对方劲力既不能到达我胸部，又不能随其意而下降，即掤劲。太极拳技击中，掤劲极为重要。

掤，八卦为坎，方位正北。

2. 捋：太极拳技击中，向旁侧横力为捋，用于借力向后引动。

对方进攻，我沾其腕肘，顺其前进之势而领向我身左或右侧，即在对方劲力之上再略加向旁侧的小力，使对方身体受到更大的旁侧方向的合力，即捋劲。

捋，八卦为离，方位正南。

3. 挤：太极拳技击中，挤住对方，使其失去运化的外推之力为挤，用于对下盘的外推。

area is.

## II. Taijiquan's Eight Types of *Jin* and Eight Techniques

Taijiquan requires one to use intention rather than force. Here the force is brute force, rather than *jin*. Taijiquan has eight types of *jin,* which all are flexible.

The eight types of *jin* are as follows.

1. Warding off: an upward silk-reeling movement by the hand;

2. Rolling back: a sideways, silk-reeling yielding movement;

3. Pressing: an upward warding off by both crossed hands;

4. Pushing: to offset with the hand, usually a slight lift up with the fingers then a push down with the palm;

5. Pulling down: to pluck or pick downwards with the hand, especially with the fingertips or palm;

6. Splitting: to separate, to twist or to offset with a spiral motion;

7. Elbowing: to strike or push with the elbow;

8. Shouldering: to strike or push with the shoulder or upper back.

Among the eight types of *jin,* Warding off is the most basic one.

The Eight Techniques of Taijiquan

The Eight Techniques of Taijiquan refer to the eight basic techniques in the attack and defense of Taijiquan: Warding off, Rolling back, Pressing, Pushing, Pulling down, Splitting, Elbowing and Shouldering, which correspond to the Eight Trigrams and eight directions respectively. Among them, Warding off, Rolling back, Pressing and Pushing are called four major methods, while Pulling down, Splitting, Elbowing and Shouldering are called four minor methods. The eight techniques are led by Warding off, with the four major methods dominating the four minor ones.

1. Warding off. It refers to an upward circular movement used to yield or offset usually with the arms to disrupt the opponent's centre of gravity in the attack and defense of Taijiquan.

The two partners form dual attached hands. When the other side makes an offensive posture with advancing hands, you respond to it with an upward and outward force, so that the other side's force can neither reach your chest nor

对敌进攻，以手、臂、肩、背粘住对方，从而向前推掷，使对方失去平衡而离开原来位置，即挤劲。

挤，八卦为震，方位正东。

4. 按：太极拳技击中，将劲力向下运动为按，用于抑制对方前进的攻击。

双方搭手，我以手向下，贯以全身之力，同时向自身牵引，使对方足跟离地，或向一侧牵引，使对方身体倾斜，即按劲。

按，八卦为兑，方位正西。

5. 採：太极拳技击中，我或一松即紧，或一落即拔，或先沉后提，或先顺后逆，意同採花摘叶，採制敌人，为採。用于迎战对方上托的劲力。

双方手肘相持或腕腕相接时，我方下沉，使对方反抗而上托，我则顺势提带使其足跟离地，即採劲。

採，八卦为乾，方位西北。

6. 挒：太极拳技击中，转移敌方劲力还制敌身为挒，用于破坏对方平衡。

对方进击，无论单手双手，我承受对方劲力同时将劲力转移对方，承受从人，顺应对方劲力方向；转移从己，改变其方向，使动作成弧状。此即挒劲。

挒，八卦为坤，方位西南。

7. 肘：太极拳技击中，以肘尖击人，称为肘。肘法极多，亦极为灵活多变。

双方接近，以肘击敌，十分锐利，极易击中肋部或其他重要部位，致敌受伤。用肘尖沉带敌方，形成牵引的劲力，也是肘法。

肘，八卦为艮，方位东北。

8. 靠：太极拳技击中，以肩背胯外侧抖、弹、撞寸劲对敌进攻为靠，双方近身时用。

descend. It is very important.

According to the Eight Trigrams, Warding off corresponds to *Kan*, which is in the due north.

2. Rolling back. It refers to a sideways, circular yielding movement used to pull the coming force backward in the attack and defense of Taijiquan.

When the opponent attacks, you touch his wrist and elbow, and lead him to the left or right side of your body as he moves forward. That is, by imposing a little force on the side of the opponent's force, the opponent's body was subject to a greater sideways force.

According to the Eight Trigrams, Rolling back corresponds to *Li*, which is in the due south.

3. Pressing. It refers to a squeezing offset in a direction away from the body.

It is usually done with the hand, the forearm, the shoulder and the back to adhere to the opponent. Then the opponent loses his balance and leaves his original position.

According to the Eight Trigrams, Pressing corresponds to *Zhen*, which is in the due east.

4. Pushing. It refers to a downward movement of the palm used to suppress the attack of the opposing party.

When the two partners attach hands, you use your hands downward. With all your force, you force the opponent's heel off the ground, or pull him sideways, so that the opponent cannot stand still.

According to the Eight Trigrams, Pushing corresponds to *Dui*, which is in the due west.

5. Pulling down. You tighten at once when being loose, or pull out when falling, or sink before lifting, or go against your opponent before going along with him. It refers to plucking or pulling the opponent downward, as if collecting or plucking flowers and leaves, which is used to fight against the lifting force from the opponent.

When the elbows or wrists of the both sides meet, you sink to make the other side resist and lift up. Then you lift the heel of the opponent off the ground.

According to the Eight Trigrams, Pulling down corresponds to *Qian*, which is in the northwest.

双方贴近，得势得机时，肩击胯打以制敌，即靠劲。时机不得而用靠，对方轻易转化，反遭敌害，故用靠切记谨慎。

靠，八卦为巽，方位东南。

6. Splitting. It refers to transferring the opponent's force, which is used to destroy the balance of the opponent.

When the opponent strikes, no matter whether it is with one hand or two hands, you bear the force of the other side while transferring the force to the opponent. You follow the direction of the opponent's force when you bear; you change its direction when transferring so as to make an arch action.

According to the Eight Trigrams, Splitting corresponds to *Kun*, which is in the southwest.

7. Elbowing. It refers to striking or pushing with the elbow. There are various and flexible methods of elbowing.

When your opponent and you are close to each other, you can attack the opponent with your elbows. They are very sharp and can easily hit the ribs or other important body parts, causing injuries to the opponent. It is also the elbowing method to use the elbow to sink the opponent and form the power of traction.

According to the Eight Trigrams, Elbowing corresponds to *Gen*, which is in the northeast.

8. Shouldering. It refers to striking or pushing with the shoulder or upper back to attack the opponent when both sides are close to each other.

When your opponent and you are close to each other, if you gain an advantage and opportunity, you should beat the opponent with your shoulders. If the opportunity is not good for you, you may easily be attacked by the opponent. Therefore, you should be cautious when using shouldering.

According to the Eight Trigrams, Shouldering corresponds to *Xun*, which is in the southeast.

第四章

# 太极拳的价值体系

---

## Chapter Ⅳ

## Functions and Values of Taijiquan

"太极拳"也被称作"哲学拳",是历代圣贤智慧的结晶。在中国古代朴素唯物辩证法和黄老学说的指导下,太极拳以哲学为理论,按照生理结构、力学原理,利用圆的运动变化将武术"踢、打、摔、拿"四大传统技法放松地隐藏其中,并独创"靠"的技法,在圆的运动中不断地练习,使人体各器官的功能得到完善发展。太极拳是用身体语言体现唯物辩证法的一种至善完美的、集养生与技击为一体的拳法,具有独特的技击、养生及其他社会功能。

## 一、太极拳的技击价值

太极拳不仅健身有法,而且技击奥妙。太极拳以掤、捋、挤、按、采、挒、肘、靠为中心内容,在粘、连、黏、随的基础上将抓、拿、摔、滑、打、跌熔为一炉,内外兼修,是武林中最优秀的拳种之一。

国家级非物质文化遗产项目太极拳代表性传承人——陈正雷

Chen Zhenglei, One of the Representative Inheritors of Taijiquan as the National Intangible Cultural Heritage

太极拳习练讲究三年一小成,九年一大成。太极拳强调虚实分明,阴阳互变,柔中带刚,刚柔并济,并且以推手检验姿势是否正确,锻炼技击技巧。练到上乘功夫,可达周身一家,以静制动,以逸代劳,以不

"Taijiquan" is also called the boxing of philosophy, which is the crystallization of the wisdom of the sages of all ages in China. Based on Chinese Ancient Naive Materialistic Dialectics and theories of the Yellow Emperor and Laozi, Taijiquan follows the principle of physiological structure and human mechanics. It adopts the circular movements to show the four traditional techniques of kicking, hitting, falling and catching and creates the technique of shouldering. Through the constant circular movements, one can improve the function of his or her various organs. Taijiquan is a kind of boxing that uses the physical body to embody materialist dialectics and integrates a regimen of the art of attack and defense as one.

## Ⅰ. The Combat Value of Taijiquan

Taijiquan is not only a way to keep fit, but also an art of attack and defense. Taijiquan adopts the eight major techniques of Warding off, Rolling back, Pressing, Pushing, Pulling down, Splitting, Elbowing and Shouldering as its center. On the basis of the basic skills of adhering, connecting, sticking, and following, it takes the skills of catching and falling as one and has become one of the best styles of boxing.

There is a saying that if you practice three years, you can get small gains; but if you practice nine years, you will make great achievement. Taijiquan focuses on the alternation of emptiness and fullness, changing between yin and yang and softness and hardness existing together. The pushing hand is adopted to check whether the posture is correct and to practice the attack skills. If the kung fu is on a high level, one will comprehend the energy and use it freely.

## Ⅱ. Health Preservation Value of Taijiquan

1. Taijiquan can improve the nervous system. The role of the nervous system is to regulate the functional activities of various organs of the body and to maintain the integrity of the internal body for adapting to the changing needs of external environment. Through the combination of mind, breathing and movement, Taijiquan promotes the perfection of brain nerve cells and coordinates the

变而应万变，亦可得机得势，舍己从人，随机应变，灵活运用，引进落空，借力打人。

## 二、太极拳的养生价值

1. 改善神经系统。神经系统的作用是调节全身各器官功能活动，保持人体内部的完整统一，以适应外部环境的变化需要。太极拳通过意念和呼吸与动作配合，促进大脑神经细胞的功能完善，使人体神经系统的兴奋和抑制过程得到协调，对精神创伤、神经类疾病，如神经衰弱、失眠、高血压等有较好的防治作用。

2. 增强心脏功能，改善循环系统，扩大肺活量。心脏病是世界第一号杀手，目前西医对这种疾病还没有特效的治疗方法，而练习太极拳能预防心脏病。这是因为太极拳不同于其他运动，它动作舒展缓慢，全身肌肉放松，既使心脏得到充足供血，又不会加快心律，加重心脏的负担。太极拳通过缓慢、细长、均匀的腹式呼吸，使人体肺部的氧气充足，肠胃得到蠕动锻炼，从而增强消化和排泄机能。所以经常锻炼太极拳，对心脏病、肺病、胃病、便秘、痔疮等有防治作用。

3. 提高人的平衡能力，防止骨质疏松。老年人常见的意外事故之一是失去平衡摔倒而导致骨折，因为老年人的骨骼钙质减少，骨质疏松。太极拳运动中，有一部分动作是专门练习平衡能力的，可使习练者的平衡能力得到充分的锻炼提高。练习太极拳时，经常用一条腿支撑全身重量，腿部受力增加，骨质的含钙量也会增加，骨骼就变得坚固。所以经常练习太极拳的人不易摔跤和骨折。

4. 具有健美作用。太极拳的顶悬、沉肩坠肘、含胸拔背、松腹开胯、敛臀等身法要求，加上在练习时的腰部旋转，可使习练者的全身肌肉得到充分锻炼，从而保持良好的体型。

processes of excitation and inhibition of the human nervous system. Therefore, it will have preventive and curative effects on psychological trauma and neurological diseases such as neurasthenia, insomnia and hypertension.

2. Taijiquan can enhance heart function, improve circulatory system and expand lung capacity. Heart disease ranks as the disease with the highest fatality rate in the world as there is no specific treatment of western medicine for this disease at present, but practicing Taijiquan can help prevent heart disease. That's because Taijiquan is different from other sports. It moves slowly and relaxes the muscles of entire body, so that the heart gets enough blood supply, but it does not speed up the heart rhythm or aggravate the burden of the heart. The slow and even abdominal breathing by practitioners allows the oxygen in the lungs of the human body to be sufficient. It also exercises the gastrointestinal motility, thus enhancing digestion and excretion function. So the Taijiquan practice has a preventive effect on heart disease, lung disease, stomach disease, constipation, hemorrhoids, etc.

3. Taijiquan can improve people's ability to balance and prevent osteoporosis. One of the common injuries in the elderly is fractures that result from a fall because the elderly have reduced bone calcium and suffer from osteoporosis. In Taijiquan practice, some of the exercises are specially designed to practice balance, through which the ability to balance of the practitioners can be fully improved. When practicing Taijiquan, we often use one leg to support the whole body's weight, the leg strength is increased, the calcium content of the bone is also increased, and the bone becomes firm. Therefore, people who often practice Taijiquan are less likely to fall and suffer fracture.

4. Taijiquan can build up bodies. The body techniques of Taijiquan, such as contracting the chest and broadening the back, lowering the shoulders and elbows and relaxing the belly, etc., plus the waist rotation during the exercise, can fully exercise the practitioner's muscles to help maintain a good physical shape.

## III. The Social Value of Taijiquan

1. The multicultural integration of Taijiquan makes it a unique window on traditional Chinese culture and a bridge for friendly exchanges with other

## 三、太极拳的社会价值

1. 太极拳的多元文化融合，使它成为展现中华传统文化的一个独特窗口，是对外友好交往的桥梁和纽带。

太极拳所蕴含的鲜明的民族特色、独特的民族特点和朴实的民族风格，不仅使它成为中华武林的一枝奇葩，同时也是中国传统文化的一种符号象征。普及、推广、保护太极拳这一文化品牌，不仅有利于继承、丰富和传播、振兴民族文化，而且可以将它作为展现中华传统文化的独特窗口，作为对外交往的桥梁和纽带，加强中国人民与世界人民的友谊，使世界人民通过习练太极拳了解中国、了解中国传统文化、了解东方文化，从而使东西方文化达成一种平衡。

2. 太极拳的多门艺术交融，有助于人们陶冶情操和对事物感觉效应的训练，丰富想象力。

太极拳的艺术性主要体现在两个方面：一是它本身具有艺术表现力，观看高水平的太极拳表演可以使人从中受到感染，从姿势优美、造型生动的拳式中感受到内在的向上激情、健康的生活信念以及对大自然的热爱和对人的尊重、宽容等。二是太极拳包含了很多其他艺术门类可以借鉴的元素。它的理论、技术和美学架构都是多元的融合，它对于节奏的处理和人的内在潜力挖掘，都有很强的艺术创作和发挥空间。

3. 太极拳对习练者的品德要求和行为规范，体现了中华民族的传统美德和高尚的道德情操，对促进中华民族认同，增强社会凝聚力，增进民族团结和社会稳定都具有十分重要的意义。

古人云"百行以德为首"，"罪莫大于无道，怨莫深于无德"。太极拳对每个演练者的武德修养有很高的要求，这也是学好太极拳的首要和必要条件。它以善与恶、丑与美、正与邪、公正与偏私、诚实与虚伪等观念来评价人们的各种行为和调整人们之间的关系。

4. 太极拳的套路和动作符合科学原理，通过周身虚实变化，使人

countries.

The distinctive national characteristic and simple national style of Taijiquan not only make it a wonderful martial art, but also a symbol of Chinese traditional culture. It will be conducive to inheriting, enriching and disseminating and revitalizing the national cultures for popularizing, promoting and protecting Taijiquan. As a unique window to showcase traditional Chinese culture and a bridge to link foreign exchanges, people in the world can learn more about Chinese culture by practicing Taijiquan, which can help create a balance between Eastern and Western Culture.

2. The multi-art feature of Taijiquan helps people to cultivate their sentiment and enrich their imagination.

The art of Taijiquan is mainly manifested in two aspects. Firstly, it has artistic expressiveness. From the beautiful postures and vivid performance, one can feel the inner passion, faith in a healthy life, love of nature and respect and tolerance for people. Secondly, Taijiquan includes many elements that other art categories can learn from. The theory, techniques and aesthetic structure of Taijiquan are all multi-integrations, which have a strong artistic creation and imaginary space for the processing of rhythm and the internal potential of human beings.

3. Taijiquan's moral requirements and behavioral norms for the practitioners fully display the traditional virtues of the Chinese nation and noble moral sentiments. They are of great significance for promoting the Chinese national identity, enhancing social cohesion, and improving national unity and social stability.

There are old sayings going like this, "virtue is the most important in different jobs" and "there is no greater sin than immorality, and there is no greater hate than immorality". Taijiquan itself has a high martial virtue requirement. This is the primary and necessary condition for learning Taijiquan. It evaluates people's behaviors and adjusts people's relationships with the concepts of good and evil, ugly and beautiful, justice and evil, justice and partiality, honesty and hypocrisy.

4. Taijiquan's routines and movements conform to scientific principles of the shift between fullness and emptiness, which can change the human body into its most favorable working state, thereby enhancing the body's immunity.

The routines and movements of Taijiquan are scientific in nature and closely

体机能处于最有利的工作状态,从而增强人体的免疫能力。

太极拳的套路和动作都具有一定的科学性,与仿生学、力学原理紧密相连。圆是自然界中最不好擒拿的物体形状了,也是最能化解来力的形状之一。太极拳则是通过太极拳顺逆缠丝的螺旋运动,来完成太极拳圆形的显象。

5. 太极拳将武术和中国养生导引之术相互融合、相互渗透,从而达到调整阴阳、疏通经络、强体健身、益寿延年的目的。

古今中外任何一种武术,其功能不外乎搏人(攻击)、御敌(防守)、健身。陈王廷在造拳的过程中自然也早有考虑,他将武术和中国养生导引之术相互融合、相互渗透,增强了太极拳的健身价值。所以,太极拳以其独特的轻柔缓慢的运动方式受到海内外人士的青睐。它松静自然、气沉丹田、中等强度的运动,不仅对心血管、呼吸系统有良好的作用,而且有利于调节神经系统,陶冶性情,缓解压力,在任何时代对社会都有着十分重要的意义。

6. 汲取百家之长的太极拳技击法,其中不但蕴含着厚重的文化、兵法内涵,而且大可以为国效力,小可以防身御侮,具有十分重要的现实意义。

武术本是一种技击,也是一种技击术。进行武术练习一方面可以全面提高人的身体素质,随着体能的增强也必然会提高进行技击对抗的能力;另一方面演练者通过武术锻炼也可以学习到许多攻防技击技术,直接提高演练者的技击对抗水平。

7. 太极拳运动富含的奥林匹克精神使它具备了丰富的国际化内涵,更有利于在世界范围内推广与全球和谐环境的营造。

太极拳是东方文化孕育的果实,奥运会是西方文化培育的盛典。仔细比较太极拳文化和奥林匹克精神,可以发现两者间有着诸多相通的理念。从运动层面比较,可以看到三个相通点:其一,两者均以身体活动为基本内容;其二,两者均能提高人体运动能力;其三,两者的最后追求都归属到了对人生哲学和生活方式的追求。

related to the principles of bionics and mechanics. The circle is the shape hardest to hold in nature. However it is one of the shapes easiest to neutralize the other party's force. Taijiquan uses a circular movement through a spiral movement to achieve a circular image.

5. Taijiquan combines martial arts with the techniques of *daoyin* from Daoism, which can achieve the purpose of adjusting yin and yang, activating meridians, strengthening physical fitness and prolonging life.

Every martial art, in China or abroad, is basically designed to attack, defense or build up body. These functions were all considered naturally in the process of creating Taijiquan by Chen Wangting. He merged martial arts and the techniques of *daoyin* of Daoism to enhance the fitness value of Taijiquan. Therefore, Taijiquan is favored by people at home and abroad for its unique gentle and slow movement. The exercise of Taijiquan is calm and natural. Its moderate exercise not only has a good influence on cardiovascular and respiratory systems, but also helps to regulate the nervous system, cultivate temperament, relieve stress, and is of great significance to society in any era.

6. Taking advantage of other martial arts, Taijiquan not only contains profound cultural and military connotation, but also can serve the country and defend against attacks. It has very important practical significance.

Martial arts are arts of attack and defense. First, martial arts exercises can comprehensively improve people's physical fitness. Consequently, with the enhancement of physical fitness, they will inevitably improve their ability to fight effectively. Second, the practitioner can also learn a lot of offensive and defensive techniques through exercises; thus, directly improving their performance.

7. The Olympic spirit in Taijiquan makes it rich in international connotation. Therefore it is more conducive to promotion of the art in the world and creation of a global harmonious environment.

Taijiquan is the symbol of Eastern culture and the Olympic Games are a grand celebration of Western culture. However, there are many similar ideas between Taijiquan culture and Olympic spirit. Through the comparison in athletic aspect, we can see three similar points: firstly, both are based on physical activity; secondly, both can improve the body's athletic ability; thirdly, the final pursuit of both is attributable to the pursuit of a philosophy of life and lifestyle.

第五章

# 太极拳的未来发展

Chapter V

The Future Development of Taijiquan

随着时代变迁和社会发展，太极拳运动也在不断蓬勃发展。作为中华传统文化精粹的太极拳，已被越来越多的人们认知和接受。

在中国国内，除去武校、武馆等专业场所，城市公园、小区、操场、路旁、河边等地，都随处可见习练太极拳的人群，甚至农村乡间的门前屋后、林荫地头，也不乏习练太极拳者的身影。在海外，无论欧亚大陆还是南北美洲、非洲、大洋洲，均能看到太极拳习练者的身姿，都能找到教练太极拳的组织机构。太极拳这枝武术百花园里的奇葩，正在百姓生活中绽放，以前所未有的兴盛和发展，渗透了社会的每个角落。

太极拳所蕴含的深奥文化内涵、奇妙健身功效以及独到的技击方法，深深吸引着全世界渴望文明、和谐、健康的人们。为了让太极拳长久兴盛不衰，更好地造福人类，太极拳的传承与发展需要得到全社会的关注和支持。

# 一、太极拳未来在中国国内的传承发展

要进一步加大对太极拳文化的保护力度，推动全国太极拳传承保护工作全面、深入地开展。未来太极拳在国内的传承发展主要集中在以下几个方面：

一是开展深入调查，建立较为完善的太极拳档案和数据库。通过开展深入的调查，了解所有太极拳文化和支脉目前的生存状况、分布区域、传承人、相关场所、实物资料、相关民俗活动、保护情况等，全面掌握其现状及存在的问题。要运用文字、图片、音像以及数字多媒体技术，对这些项目进行全面系统的记录、整理，收集相关代表性实物，予以妥善保存，并建立档案及相关数据库。

二是分类指导，科学保护。中国太极拳文化发展迅速，支脉较多，拳理虽然相通，但技术特点各异。目前国家级名录扩展项目已有

Taijiquan is also constantly developing with the changes that occur over time and other social developments. As an essence of Chinese traditional culture, it has been recognized and accepted by an increasing number of people.

Apart from professional schools such as martial arts schools and martial arts halls, people who practice Taijiquan can be seen everywhere in China, for instance: in urban parks, communities, playgrounds, roadsides, riversides, even in front of the rural countryside and in the shade of the trees. We can also see the Taijiquan practitioners and find the organizations of Taijiquan in Eurasia, North America, South America, Africa and Oceania. As a miracle of Chinese Wushu, Taijiquan is blooming in the lives of the people and infiltrating into every corner of society with an unprecedented speed.

The profound cultural connotation, wonderful fitness effects and unique methods of Taijiquan have deeply attracted people who are eager for civilization, harmony and good health in the world. However, the inheritance and development of Taijiquan needs the support of the whole society in order to make Taijiquan prosper for a long time and better benefit mankind.

# Ⅰ. The Future Development of Taijiquan in China

It is necessary to further strengthen the protection of Taijiquan culture and promote the comprehensive and deep development of Taijiquan's inheritance. The future development of Taijiquan in China mainly focuses on the following aspects:

Firstly, a relatively complete Taijiquan archives and database should be established through a thorough investigation. Through a thorough investigation, we will understand the current living conditions, distribution areas, holders, related places, physical materials, related folk activities, and the status of Taijiquan culture and its branches, and comprehensively grasp the current situation and existing problems. It is necessary to use text, pictures, audio and video and digital multimedia technology to systematically record and organize these items, collect relevant representative objects, preserve them properly and establish archives and related databases.

Secondly, we should classify each style according to its type and protect each

陈氏太极拳、杨氏太极拳、武氏太极拳、孙氏太极拳、吴氏太极拳、李氏太极拳、王其和太极拳、和氏太极拳等。因此，应根据分类指导的原则，因地制宜地开展保护工作。

太极拳发源地——中国河南省温县陈家沟太极拳展演活动
A Taijiquan Performance in the Birthplace of Taijiquan, Chenjiagou Village, Wenxian County, Henan Province, China

三是加强对太极拳代表性传承人的保护，建立有效的传承机制。传承人是太极拳的重要承载者和传承者，加强对传承人的保护，是太极拳保护工作和传承发展的关键。因此，我们要继续对太极拳项目代表性传承人进行认定、命名，不仅要为其出书立传，而且要为其开展太极拳传习活动提供必要的传承场所，资助其开展授徒传艺、教学、交流等活动，并对太极拳传承工作有突出贡献的代表性传承人给予表彰、奖励。同时对学艺者采取助学、奖学的鼓励方式，以培养更多的后继人才。与教育部门合作，将太极拳有关知识纳入大中小学相关课程或教学内容，推进太极拳进课堂、进教材、进校园。利用公共文化

style in a scientific way. The Chinese Taijiquan culture develops rapidly and has many branches. Although the theory is the same, the technical characteristics are different. At present, the national directory extension project has Chen style Taijiquan, Yang style Taijiquan, Wu style Taijiquan, Sun style Taijiquan, Woo style Taijiquan, Li style Taijiquan, Wang Qihe style Taijiquan and He style Taijiquan. Therefore, the protection should be carried out according to the principles of each different type.

Thirdly, we should strengthen the protection of the representative holders of Taijiquan and establish an effective inheritance mechanism. As we know, the holders play an important role in Taijiquan promotion, and strengthening the protection of the holders is the key to the inheritance of Taijiquan. Therefore, we must continue to identify and name the representative holders of the Taijiquan project, including writing biographies for them, providing necessary inheritance sites for the Taijiquan training activities, funding their teaching and communication and rewarding the representative holders who have made outstanding contributions to the inheritance of Taijiquan. At the same time, scholars should be encouraged to award scholarships to train more lineage holders. We should cooperate with the education department, making the relevant knowledge of Taijiquan incorporated into the relevant courses or teaching contents of the schools, promoting Taijiquan into the classroom, the textbook and the campus. We can also provide social education on Taijiquan culture for the public by using public cultural facilities to carry out lectures, training and other activities.

Fourthly, we should increase the investment in Taijiquan protection and provide financial security. The implementation of funds is an important guarantee for the protection of Taijiquan. Since 2004, China's central government has set up a special fund to support the protection of national intangible cultural heritage projects including Taijiquan. At the same time, we must urge all localities to implement the corresponding supporting funds to ensure that the Taijiquan protection funds are in place. In addition, we must also expand investment channels and actively absorb social forces to participate in the protection of Taijiquan.

Fifthly, we should strengthen infrastructure construction and encourage

设施，开展讲座、培训等活动，面向社会公众开展太极拳文化的社会教育。

四是加大太极拳保护投入力度，提供资金保障。落实资金是开展太极拳保护工作的重要保障。从2004年开始，中国中央财政已专门设立非物质文化遗产专项资金，支持包括太极拳在内的国家级非物质文化遗产名录项目的保护工作。同时，要督促各地落实相应的配套资金，确保太极拳保护经费落实到位。此外，也要扩大投入渠道，积极吸纳社会力量参与太极拳传承保护工作。

五是加强基础设施建设，鼓励兴建太极拳展示传习场所。要将太极拳的展示与传习基础设施建设纳入公共文化服务体系建设和当地经济、社会发展规划，建设一批太极拳专题展示馆和传习所。鼓励企事业组织、社会团体以及其他组织和个人设立相关的太极拳专题博物馆、传习所。通过加强基础设施建设，一方面展示相关的太极拳实物资料，另一方面也为太极拳代表性传承人开展活态展示和组织传习活动提供场所，增强民众对非物质文化遗产太极拳的了解和认识，使太极拳专题博物馆或传习所成为对青少年进行传统文化教育的重要载体。

六是合理利用太极拳文化资源，促进传承发展。要积极促进太极拳文化资源的合理开发和利用，推动太极拳的传承发展。加紧研究有关产业政策，制定融资、税收等方面的优惠政策，鼓励和支持各地对合理利用太极拳发展文化产业的企业等经营单位予以扶持，并积极探索太极拳文化遗产保护与旅游发展、社会主义新农村建设相结合的途径，为经济、社会全面协调可持续发展做贡献。

七是开展科研教育，加强太极拳人才培训。要积极鼓励开展与太极拳有关的科学、技术研究和保护方法研究，充分发挥有关研究机构和大专院校的作用，鼓励建立相应的太极拳文化研究机构或社会团体，命名一批太极拳文化遗产研究基地，利用国内外学术研讨会、交流会等方式，推动太极拳相关理论研究和政策研究的深入。通过组织

the construction of Taijiquan exhibition venues. It is necessary to incorporate Taijiquan's display and training infrastructure into the construction of public cultural service system and local economic and social development plans, and to build a number of Taijiquan special exhibition halls. The enterprises, institutions, social organizations, and other organizations and individuals are encouraged to set up relevant Taijiquan special museums and exhibition venues. The strengthening of infrastructure construction, on the one hand will display the relevant material objects, on the other hand, it will also provide a venue for the Taijiquan representative holders to carry out live demonstrations and organize training activities. This will enhance the public's understanding of Taijiquan and make the Taijiquan special museum or exhibition venue become an important carrier for traditional cultural education for young people.

Sixthly, we should make rational use of Taijiquan cultural resources and promote its development. We need to intensify research on industrial policies, formulate preferential policies on financing and taxation, encourage and support local enterprises to develop cultural industries, and actively explore Taijiquan cultural heritage protection and tourism development and the combination of new rural construction, which will contribute to the overall coordinated and sustainable development of the economy and society.

Seventhly, we should carry out scientific research and education and strengthen the training of Taijiquan talents. We should actively encourage research on the science, technique research and protection methods related to Taijiquan, give full play to the role of relevant research institutions and universities, encourage the establishment of corresponding Taijiquan culture research institutions or social groups, name a group of Taijiquan cultural heritage research bases, and promote the theoretical research and policy research of Taijiquan by means of academic seminars and exchanges at home and abroad. Taijiquan protection staff should also be trained to improve their professional skills and working competence through training courses, on-site study and experience exchange, etc. At the same time, some relevant colleges or research institutions are entrusted to train a group of high-level Taijiquan cultural heritage protection professionals.

Eighthly, we should advance the legislative process and formulate

培训班、现场考察学习、经验交流等方式，经常对现有太极拳保护工作人员进行业务培训，提高其业务水平和工作能力；同时，委托相关大专院校或研究机构，培养一批高层次的太极拳文化传承保护专业人才。

八是推进立法进程，制定相应保护政策。2011年6月1日起，《中华人民共和国非物质文化遗产保护法》开始执行，并鼓励各地出台相关的非物质文化遗产保护条例或专项保护法规，为太极拳的传承保护提供法律保障。根据各地区太极拳传承的具体情况，有针对性地制定出台相应的保护扶持政策，推动太极拳传承保护工作深入持续地开展。

九是广泛开展宣传展示活动，促进非物质文化遗产太极拳的传播和弘扬。通过广播、影视、报刊、互联网等大众传媒，积极报道宣传太极拳的保护工作；鼓励各种传播机构拍摄制作与太极拳相关的视听节目或音像制品，组织相关保护成果的出版；鼓励图书馆、文化馆、博物馆、科技馆和非物质文化遗产学术研究机构、保护机构等，开展太极拳的整理、研究、宣传、展示活动和学术交流活动。结合文化遗产日和民族传统节日，广泛开展健康有益的活动，普及太极拳知识，促进太极拳的传播，增强全社会传承弘扬太极拳文化的意识，为太极拳传承发展营造良好的社会氛围。

中国太极拳的传承发展是一个系统工程，它既受国家体育政策和自身文化价值功能的制约，也受到当地经济发展、社会体育参与以及组织制度问题的影响。未来太极拳在国内的传承发展趋势与推广模式，可以根据太极拳自身所具有的价值和功能来确定。

太极拳是中国武术发展历程中诞生的一个优秀拳种，也是目前在国内开展最广泛、普及度最高、知名度最大的武术运动项目之一，是中华武术的"金字招牌"。它具有丰富的内涵，不仅赋予了国人良好的精神风貌和民族形象，更是华夏民族精神建构的脊梁。

除了竞技太极拳之外，众多的太极拳习练者所追求的理念基本是

corresponding protection policies. Since June 1, 2011, *Law on the Protection of Intangible Cultural Heritage of People's Republic of China* has been implemented, and local goverments have been encouraged to issue relevant intangible cultural heritage protection regulations or special protection laws to provide legal protection for the inheritance and protection of Taijiquan. According to the specific situation of Taijiquan inheritance in various regions, the corresponding protection and support policies are formulated, and the work of inheritance and protection is promoted in an in-depth and continuous manner.

Ninthly, we should carry out extensive displaying activities to promote the spread of Taijiquan. We can actively support the protection of Taijiquan through the mass media such as radio, film, newspapers and the internet, and by encouraging various communication agencies to produce audio-visual programs or audio-visual products related to Taijiquan, organizing the publication of relevant protection results, encouraging libraries, cultural centers, museums, science museums, academic research institutions and protection institutions for intangible cultural heritage to carry out Taijiquan's documents collection, research, publicity, exhibition activities and academic exchange events. In combination with cultural heritage days and national traditional festivals, we will popularize Taijiquan knowledge, promote the spread of Taijiquan, enhance the awareness of the whole society to carry forward the culture of Taijiquan and create a good social atmosphere for the development of Taijiquan.

The inheritance and development of Chinese Taijiquan is a systematic project. It is not only restricted by the national sports policy and its own cultural value function, but also affected by local economic development, social sports participation and organizational system issues. The future development trend and promotion mode of Taijiquan in China can be determined according to the value and function of Taijiquan itself.

Taijiquan is an excellent boxing type of Chinese martial arts and one of the most extensive, popular and well-known martial arts in China, which is one of the most famous symbols of Chinese martial arts. It has a rich connotation, which gives the Chinese people a good spiritual outlook and national image; moreover, it is the backbone of the Chinese national spirit.

In addition to competitive Taijiquan, the concepts pursued by many Taijiquan

一致的：太极拳在青少年中秉承着"习拳育人，塑造人格"的教育理念，也成为中老年人"休闲娱乐，健身健心"的主要运动方式。耳闻"太极"两字，就寓意出健身养生之观念，这一观念已深深地烙在了广大民众的心里，健身养生理念在人们心中早已根深蒂固。太极拳已成为人们锻炼身体的最佳选择和休闲娱乐的方式之一。因此，太极拳在中国有着深厚的群众基础，有着基数庞大的参与人群。

太极拳发源地——中国河南省温县陈家沟太极拳演练
The Daily Practice of Taijiquan in Chenjiagou, Wenxian County, Henan Province of China

为充分发挥太极文化之优势，满足社会民生之需求，让太极拳更好地服务社会，造福人民，未来太极拳可从三个方面进行传承发展。

一是以合作化模式进行传承推广。太极拳具有多元化价值功能，适合采用"合作式"发展推广模式，面向企事业单位、医疗机构、商业性组织等推广自身价值品牌。

1. 向企事业单位推广。国家的兴盛、民族的强健、社会的进步、经济的发展皆取决于人，取决于人的素质。而劳动者的身体素质，则

practitioners are basically the same: young people adhere to the educational concept of educating people and shaping personality while middle-aged and elderly people adopt the mode of exercise for entertainment, fitness and health. Taijiquan is a symbol of fitness and health. This concept has been deeply branded in the hearts of the general public. Taijiquan has become the best choice for people to exercise and one of the lifestyles of entertainment. Therefore, Taijiquan has a deep mass base in China and has a large number of participants.

In order to give full play to the advantages of Taijiquan culture and meet the needs of the people's livelihood, Taijiquan can be inherited from three aspects to serve the society better and benefit the people in the future.

Firstly, we should inherit and promote Taijiquan in a cooperative model. Taijiquan has diversified functions. Therefore we can adopt a cooperative development model to promote its own value brand for enterprises, institutions, medical institutions and commercial organizations.

1. To promote it in enterprises and institutions. The prosperity of the country, the strength of the nation, the progress of society and the development of the economy depend on the quality of people. The physical quality of the workers is the basis of their ideological and moral qualities. The reason why the country attaches so much importance to the fitness of the whole nation is that the strong person is the guarantee to a strong country. The national fitness movement conforms to the trend of the times and the will of the people; therefore, it will surely benefit the society and the people. The Taijiquan culture that is contending for a hundred schools has rich health value, education value, entertainment value and economic value, which is in line with the value needs of the company's culture. The economy is developing rapidly, and large and medium-sized companies are gradually increasing nowadays. This group is a core component of the country's economic development. As profit is the developmental goal of enterprises, the competition is becoming increasingly fierce. Therefore there is always the principle of natural selection and survival of the fittest. The public institution is a service agency with government functions and serving the society as its main purpose, and with a certain public welfare nature, mainly engaged in education, science and technology, culture, health and other activities. The branches of various industries included in the public institutions are extremely extensive, which open

是其思想道德素质和科学文化素质的基础。国家之所以如此重视全民健身，是因为"强国必先强种，天生万物，唯人为贵"。全民健身运动顺应时代潮流，合乎民心民意，必将"育万民之力，兴千秋之业，造百代之强，立永世之功"。百家争鸣的太极拳文化具有丰富的健身养生价值、教育价值、娱乐价值及经济价值等，契合广大公司企业文化生存的价值需求。当今社会，经济发展迅速，大中小型公司企业逐步增加。该群体是国家经济发展的核心组成部分。企业的发展主要是以营利为目的，其相互竞争日趋激烈，"物竞天择，适者生存"的法则始终存在。而事业单位是以政府职能、服务社会为主要宗旨，并带有一定的公益性质的服务机构，主要从事教育、科技、文化、卫生等活动。事业单位所包含的各行各业的分支机构单位极为广泛，这也为太极拳的推广和普及开拓了更广阔的发展空间。但是，太极拳在企事业单位的推广，必须抓住两者的所需所求，然后依据太极拳价值为企事业单位创造更高的价值，达到"互利共赢、同步发展"的目的。这就是"合作"的经营之道。

2. 向保健医疗机构推广。人类健康是一定时代、社会发展成果在人类生命质量上的综合反映。目前，我国正在进入一个社会经济繁荣与公民健康退化如影相随的时期，人民群众看病难、看病贵的问题日益突出，以及由此而形成的医生、医院、医疗的"三医"问题，已经逐步成为不亚于"三农"问题的社会弊端。医疗服务领域所出现的这些问题亟待完善，所面临的挑战也不容回避。太极拳和人类生命的有机融合，在强身健体、益寿延年、防病治病上发挥其更大的作用，更好、更加广泛地服务于人类社会，是我们必须研究和探索的永恒的主题。太极拳运动不仅对人体具有强身健体、防病治病的良好作用，而且作为医疗体育手段，具有极大的医疗保健价值。

3. 商业化推广。随着城市经济的蓬勃发展，广大市民生活水平日趋提高和闲暇时间的增多，人们对健康的追求也与日俱增，"花钱买

up a broader space for the promotion and popularization of Taijiquan. However, the promotion of Taijiquan in enterprises and institutions must meet their needs. Then, according to the value of Taijiquan, we will create higher value for enterprises and institutions, and achieve the goal of mutual benefit and win-win development. This is the way to cooperate.

2. To promote it in health care institutions. Human health is a comprehensive reflection of the achievements of a certain era and social development in the quality of human life. At present, China is entering a period of social and economic prosperity and a deterioration of citizens' health. The problem of the difficulty in seeing a doctor and expensive medical treatment has become increasingly prominent. The resulting three medical issues, including affordable doctors, hospitals and medical care have gradually become social problems that are no less important than the three rural issues (agriculture, rural areas and rural people). The problems in medical services need to be improved, and the challenges they face can not be avoided. The organic integration of Taijiquan and human life plays an even greater role in strengthening the body, prolonging life, preventing disease and treating diseases. It will be an eternal theme in serving the human society better and more widely. Taijiquan not only has a good effect on the body, but also has great health care value as a medical care and sports supplement.

3. To promote it in commercialized way. The daily living standards of the general public, leisure time and people's pursuit of health have increased along with the vigorous development of the urban economy. The consumption related to health has become the most important consumption concept of the masses. Commercial sports and fitness clubs appeared on every corner of the city quickly in the late 1990s. Nowadsys, commercial promotion and development models such as physical fitness clubs and health clubs have become a mainstream industry conforming to social needs. They can provide the need for the harmonious development of urban society as well as services for public fitness and entertainment, thus guiding the public to change the concept of sports and fitness consumption, and enhancing the public awareness of sports and fitness consumption.

Secondly, we should follow the service model for inheritance and promotion. With the service-oriented promotion model, Taijiquan will enter the school and

健康"已成为大众的最主要消费观念。20世纪90年代末,商业性体育健身俱乐部像雨后春笋般出现在各城市的每个角落,如今,体育健身会所、养生馆及健身俱乐部等商业化推广发展模式,已成为社会需求的主流行业,在满足城市社会和谐发展需要的同时,也为大众的健身娱乐提供服务,并进一步引导着市民体育健身消费观念的转变,增强市民进行体育健身消费的意识。

太极拳发源地——中国河南省温县陈家沟太极拳演练

The Daily Practice of Taijiquan in Chenjiagou, Wenxian County, Henan Province of China

二是以服务化模式进行传承推广。通过"服务性"推广模式,使太极拳走进学校,走进社区。新时期太极拳的传承与发展要锁定推广对象与普及范围,落实以不同年龄、地位阶级、群体为着重点。

1. 走进社区。随着中国社会主义市场经济体制的改革和基层社会结构的逐步调整,社区的地位和作用显得越来越重要。社区体育服务

the community. In the new era, the inheritance and development of Taijiquan should focus on a promotion target and popularization enlargement scope, and focus on different ages, social classes and groups.

1. Taijiquan should enter into the community. The community has become increasingly important along with the reform of China's socialist market economic system and the gradual adjustment of grassroots social structure. Community sports service is an important part of community construction and community service, especially the requirements of community residents to pursue quality of life and build a harmonious community that enable community public sports services to flourish. The ageing population was defined at the 37th session of the United Nations General Assembly in 1982 that people began to enter old age at the age of 60. If the over-60-year-olds account for 10% of the total population, or the over-65-year-olds for 7% of the total in a country or region, it will be called ageing. According to this standard, China has become a veritable ageing country and a large country with an ageing population. It is estimated that by 2050, the number of elderly people in China will rise to 400 million. Faced with these amazing numbers and phenomena, the promotion of Taijiquan in the community is even more urgent because it is one of the best projects for lifelong physical exercise.

2. Taijiquan should enter into the school. The school is a holy place for teaching and educating people, and a source of cultural communication. The development of any kind of culture is inseparable from school education. In order to maintain the long-term development, it is necessary to carry out Taijiquan in schools more deeply and extensively. After the founding of People's Republic of China, Taijiquan and Changquan successively entered the physical education textbooks for readers ranging from pupils to college students. On April 3, 2004, *The Outline for the Implementation of the National Spirit Education in Primary and Secondary Schools* was issued by the Central Committee of the Communist Party of China, which clearly stated that Chinese martial arts should be added into sports classes. Besides, the outline of teaching guidance for wushu curriculum in *Teaching Guidance of Main Courses of P.E. Undergraduate Program in China's Institutions of Higher Learning* was issued by the General Office of the Ministry of Education, which clarified the status of martial arts in school

是社区建设和社区服务的重要组成部分，特别是广大社区居民追求生活质量和建设"和谐社区"的要求，使社区公共体育服务得到了蓬勃发展。1982年联合国召开的第37届联合国大会对老龄人口进行了界定，人在60岁左右就开始进入老年期。一个国家和地区60岁以上的人口数量占总人口的10%，或者是65岁以上的人口数量占总人口的7%，都将被称为"老龄化的"国家或地区。按照这一标准，中国已经成为名副其实的老龄型国家，而且是老龄人口大国。预计到2050年，中国的老龄人口数量将上升到4亿。面对这些惊人的数字和现象，太极拳在社区的推广更显急迫，毕竟它是终身体育锻炼的最佳项目之一。

2. 走进学校。学校是教书育人的圣地，是传播文化的源头，任何一种文化的发展都离不开学校教育。因此，要想使太极拳保持传播发展的长久态势，就要让学校的太极拳教育开展得更深入广泛。中华人民共和国成立后，太极拳、长拳先后进入大、中、小学的体育教材。2004年4月3日，中共中央颁发了《中小学开展弘扬和培育民族精神教育实施纲要》并明确指出："体育课应适量增加中国武术等内容。"以及教育部制定的《体育课程标准》和教育部办公厅印发的《普通高等学校体育教育本科专业各类主干课程教学指导纲要》里的"武术类课程教学指导纲要"中，都明确了武术在学校体育中的地位。学校的社会职能是培养体育人才、发展体育科学，并直接为社会服务和引领文化潮流。目前，太极拳已成为人类社会追求健康的标志和品牌。所以，要借国家颁发教育规章制度的契机，把太极拳作为武术的特色推广到学校去，试行开设阳光体育特色课程。这不仅是培养新一代学生进行民族文化教育的理想途径，也是新时期构造社会主义文化强国的重要突破口。

三是以生活化模式进行传承推广。在各地成立社区太极拳协会，使社区体育与学校体育紧密结合；开拓"太极生活化与生活太极化"互转型路线，坚守"从生活中来，到生活中去"的实践战略。

sports. The social function of school is to train sports talents, develop sports science, directly serve the society and lead the cultural trend. At present, Taijiquan has become a symbol for human society to pursue health. Therefore, it should be promoted to the school as a special martial art by taking the opportunity of issuing educational rules and regulations by the state. This is not only an ideal way to train a new generation of students to carry out national cultural education, but also an important breakthrough in building a strong socialist culture in the new era.

Thirdly, Taijiquan should be promoted in our daily life. The Community Taijiquan Association should be established in various places to make community sports and school sports closely integrated. We can also open up the mutual transformation path that Taijiquan is part of our daily life and vice versa.

With the accelerated pace of life and increased work pressure, people's psychological ability to cope is constantly under stress. Therefore, human life needs the cultivation of Taiji spirit and Taijiquan also needs to enter into life, that is "Taiji life", which refers to the fact that people should follow the philosophical theory of Taijiquan in daily life's law, rhythms, paces, habits, etc. Some theories, for example, opposition of yin and yang, balance between hardness and softness, and storing energy firstly and then releasing it, are the philosophies that help adjust people's best psychological state in life, work and study. The idea that hardness and softness exist together should be applied to deal with people and things. Moreover the hardness and softness should be manifested on different occasions, for different people and different things, but the two premises must be combined. In other words, it means to maintain balance or coordination between each other in the process of communicating with others; that is, everything must be in a certain degree. It is inevitable that misunderstanding and conflict will occur between superiors and subordinates and among colleagues, therefore, we can follow the Taiji principle of advancing and retreating in an orderly manner and hardness and softness exist together to maintain the relationship. The concept of storing energy firstly and then releasing it and advocating yin and softness not only reflects the combat characteristics of Taijiquan, but also reflects the unique concept of civilized communication of the East. *Zhongyong(Golden Mean)* mentioned, "The equilibrium is the great root from which grow all the human

随着生活节奏的加快,工作压力加大,人们心理承受能力却不断降低。因此,人类生活需要太极化,太极拳的发展更需要迈入生活化。"太极生活",是指人们在日常生活中的规律、节奏、步伐、习惯等,都应遵循太极拳学中的哲学理论,如阴阳对立、刚柔并济、先蓄后发等,都是帮助人们在生活、工作、学习中调整到最佳心理状态的哲理。包括为人处世,也应讲究"刚柔并济",在不同场合,针对不同人、不同事,做出"刚与柔"的情绪表现,但两者的前提必须是"并济",并济就是在与人相处交流的过程中,保持彼此间关系的平衡或协调,也就是说凡事都要把握个"度",即适可而止。像上级与下属、同事与同事之间,难免会发生摩擦和冲突,为了不伤害彼此的关系,就必须遵循"进退有序,刚柔相济"的太极原理。其"后发制人""崇尚阴柔"的观念,不仅体现了太极拳的技击风格特点,从某种社会生活程度上也体现了东方人独特的文明交际理念。《中庸》有云:"中也者,天下之大本也;和也者,天下之达道也。致中和,天地位焉,万物育焉。"儒家也强调"中"是天下根本,天下本源,万物只有达到"中和"的状态,方能和谐平稳发展。和谐中庸的生活方式造就了"尚中贵和"的精神状态与处世原则。

太极拳在大众生活中经过不断地"去陈推新""提炼发展",逐步形成了融哲理、拳理、医理于一身,并具有健身、修心、养性、娱乐、休闲等多元化功能的传统体育项目。太极拳把人们的健身理念、生活方式巧妙地融合了"人与自然""人与人"间的和谐宇宙观、世界观,是追求极限、打破自然的西方体育文化所无法比拟的。如今太极拳的"生活化"发展,其作用不仅体现在人文精神和社会主义精神文明建设方面,也是抵御文化垃圾对人们生活方式、思想观念腐蚀的重要工具。太极拳从道家汲取了顺应自然的思想,倡导人与自然、人与人、人与社会间的和谐共处。人类在长期的生活实践过程中,在不断地与人、与社会、与自然建立着交往关系,其之间不能简单地归

acting in the world, and this harmony is the universal path which they all should pursue. Let the states of equilibrium and harmony exist in perfection, and a happy order will prevail throughout heaven and earth, and all things will be nourished and flourish." Confucianism also emphasizes that equilibrium is the origin of the world, and all things can achieve a harmonious and stable development under the condition of balanced harmony. The equilibrium and harmony lifestyle fosters the mental condition and principles of advocating harmony.

In the public life, Taijiquan has gradually formed as a traditional sport with a combination of philosophy, boxing and medical science through continuous refined development, owning a diversified function of fitness, cultivation, nourishment, entertainment and recreation. Taijiquan blends the harmonious cosmology and worldviews between man and nature and between man and man in people's fitness concept and lifestyle. Therefore, it is unmatched by western sports culture in pursuit of the limit and breaking the nature. Nowadays, the development of Taijiquan towards life highlights an important system of humanistic spirit and socialist spiritual civilization construction, which is also an important tool to resist the erosion caused by the cultural wastes of people's lifestyles and ideas. Taijiquan took the idea of conforming to nature from Daoism and advocated the harmonious coexistence between man and nature, man and man and man and society. In the long-term practice, human beings have established relationships with people, society and nature. The relationship can't be defined as conquering and being conquered, but should be a two-way harmonious coexistence. In the current social life, the value of harmony needs to be rooted in Chinese people's way of thinking. A new type of relationship would be established in line with Taijiquan's idea "harmony between man and nature" and "focusing on neutralization", which pursues symbiosis, coexistence and common development between man and nature, man and society, man and man.

Therefore, the future development of Taijiquan will not only be of great significance for cultivating the Chinese national spirit, promoting Chinese civilization, and building a spiritual home for the Chinese nation, but also play an

为征服与被征服的关系，而应是双向度的和谐共处关系。在当前的社会生活环境下，和谐的价值理念更需要植根于我国人们的思维方式之中，用太极拳一贯秉承的"天人合一"和"尚中贵和"的思维方式，追求人与自然、与社会、与人之间共生、共存、共同发展的新型关系。

因此，未来做好太极拳的传承发展工作，不仅对培育中华民族精神、弘扬中华文明、建设中华民族共有精神家园具有重要意义，而且对于保持世界文化多样性、促进国际社会文明对话、实现人类社会可持续发展都具有重要作用。

## 二、太极拳未来在国际上的传承发展

健康是人类生活永恒的追求话题，休闲、健身、运动、娱乐是21世纪阳光体育的发展趋势，同样也是21世纪开拓新型生活方式的新理念。

太极拳以柔克刚、以静待动、以圆化直、以小胜大、以弱胜强的特点，是武术和兵法的有机结合。太极拳具有技击防身、健身养生、表演娱乐、传承文化等价值，习练太极拳不仅可以强身健体、攻防格斗，还能够修身养性。经过对人体医学、生理、生化、解剖、心理、力学等多学科的研究发现，太极拳对防治高血压、心脏病、肺病、肝炎、关节病、胃肠病、神经衰弱等慢性病均有很好的疗效。因此，太极拳备受人们青睐。

important role in maintaining world cultural diversity, promoting dialogue among international civilizations and realizing the sustainable development of human society.

## II. The Inheritance and Development of Taijiquan in the International Community

Health is the eternal pursuit of human life. Recreation, fitness, sports and entertainment are the sports development trends of the 21st century. They are also a new concept of developing new lifestyles in the 21st century.

Taijiquan is a combination of martial arts and the art of war with the characteristics of overcoming hardness with softness, coping with attackers' motion by remaining motionless and defeating the strong by the weak, etc. Taijiquan has the values of self-defense, fitness and health preservation, entertainment, and the inheritance of culture, etc. It can not only strengthen the body, attack and defend, but also own the function of self-cultivation. After research on human medicine, physiology, biochemistry, anatomy, psychology, mechanics and other multidisciplinary studies, Taijiquan has a good effect on prevention and treatment of hypertension, heart disease, lung disease, hepatitis, joint disease, gastroenteropathy, neurasthenia and other chronic diseases. Therefore, Taijiquan is well received by people.

Taijiquan combines traditional Chinese culture such as yin and yang, Confucianism, Daoism, traditional Chinese medicine meridian with techniques of traditional martial arts. It has a long history, profound spirit and diversified value function. It is a harmonious and healthy symbol for the people, highlighting the common core value orientation of the Chinese nation. It can meet the needs of modern people's fitness and health.

A. H. Maslow, an American scholar, once proposed that once one need is satisfied, another need will emerge and be satisfied as human needs appear in the form of hierarchy. The diversified development of Taijiquan fits the diverse needs of the mass. As the life of the public needs a level from the perspective of behavioral analysis, people constantly propose different, multi-faceted and multi-level needs based on their living condition and social status. Everyone needs to

中国太极拳博物馆
Taijiquan Museum of China

太极拳是融合了太极阴阳、儒家思想、道家思想、中医经络学等中华传统文化，并在此影响下与传统武技相结合而产生的，具有源远流长的历史，拥有博大浩然之精气，携带多元化价值功能。太极拳为人类社会打造了和谐健康的品牌，突显了中华民族共同的核心价值取向。它可以满足现代人们健身、养生的需要。

美国学者马斯洛曾经提出："人的需要是以层次的形式出现的，一旦一种需要被满足，另一种需要就会出现，并要求满足。"太极拳多元化的发展趋势契合大众多元化的生活需求。从行为学视角来分析，大众的生活需要层次，是根据各自的生活贫富程度、身份地位，来不断地提出不同的、多方面的、多层次需求。人人都要生活，生活需要健康，需要快乐，需要文明，更需要文化。太极拳运动"绿色、低碳、环保"的体育健身特点，使它不受场地、经济、政府、政策的制约。从社会学角度分析，大众生活文化的形成、主动性的大众消费是人们从众心理的反映。抓住大众心理，满足大众生活需求，就是大

live on the earth; however life needs health, happiness, civilization and culture. Taijiquan is a physical fitness characterized by "being green, low-carbon and being environmentally friendly". It is not subject to the constraints of the venue, economy, government and policy. From the perspective of sociology, the active mass consumption is a reflection of people's herd mentality. The most direct driving force for the public is grasping the public's psychology and satisfying the needs of the masses of life. The activities of the masses should be the main force in the development of society.

The future development of Taijiquan in the world should be considered from the aspects of competitive competition and folk heritage. In competitive competitions, the following aspects should be taken into consideration.

Firstly, it should be in line with the Olympic standards. As the cultural development strategy of China in the past 10 years, the internationalization of Taijiquan has been vigorously promoted as a competitive sports event or a mass sports project. At present, the international process of Taijiquan is taking steps to the stage of standardization. In recent years, relevant individuals of the International Wushu Federation are keenly aware of the importance of standardization and are determined to build a high-level platform to promote the Taijiquan project as an independent event. This is a very important decision in the development of martial arts. In 2014, the first World Taijiquan Championship was held in Chengdu.

Therefore, from the perspective of competition, it must be in line with the Olympic Games competition standards in the World Taijiquan Championships, where the application of certain competition rules, technical systems, judgment standards and modern information means should be as good as or better than that in the similar projects of the Olympic Games.

Secondly, Taijiquan should set new items. The new World Taijiquan Championship will be a new attempt from the project settings. First of all, the self-selected items include self-selected Taijiquan, self-selected Taiji sword; followed by the prescribed items include Chen style Taijiquan, Chen style Taiji sword, Yang style Taijiquan, Yang style Taiji sword; in addition, there are collective items, including 6 people of collective boxing sword (three men practice boxing and three women practice swords). Therefore the basic elements of the Taiji

众为之消费的最直接推动力，大众群体所参与的活动应是主流社会发展的主力军。

太极拳未来在国际间的传承发展要从竞技比赛和民间传承两方面考虑。在竞技比赛上，需要注意以下几个问题。

一是与奥运标准接轨。太极拳国际化作为我国近10年来的文化发展战略，无论是作为竞技体育项目还是大众体育项目，都在着力推进实施中，目前太极拳的国际化正处于标准化阶段。近年来，国际武联相关人士敏锐地意识到标准化的重要性，决心打造一个高水平的平台，将太极拳项目拿出来作为一个独立赛事进行推广，这是武术发展进程中非常重要的一个决策。2014年，首届世界太极拳锦标赛在成都举办。

因此，在世界太极拳锦标赛中，从竞赛的角度讲，必须要和奥运会的竞赛标准相接轨，某些竞赛规则、技术体系、评判标准、现代化信息手段的应用，要与奥运会同类项目媲美甚至超越它们。

二是项目设置新尝试。新的世界太极拳锦标赛将从项目设置上进行新尝试。首先在自选项目上，包括自选太极拳、自选太极剑；其次是规定项目，包括陈氏太极拳、陈氏太极剑，杨氏太极拳、杨氏太极剑；另外还有集体项目，包括6人的集体拳剑（男子3人练拳、女子3人练剑）。在这样的一个项目结构体系中，自选、规定、集体项目中的太极拳拳式、剑式的基本元素和规则中的竞赛体系，必须要保持一致性、标准化。

研究项目设置时，主要在传统的杨氏、陈氏以及其他拳种的原型中找到其最传统的元素，并且征求民间拳师的意见，构建标准的技术体系。在新的竞赛体系中，运动员选择的每一个动作都有价值。而过去，运动员的很多类似动作并没有价值，反而蹦、跳这些难度动作有很高价值。未来这种现象不复存在，这将使武术的传统得到更好的继承和发扬。

routines and sword styles in the self-selected items, prescribed items and collective items and the rules of competition system must be consistent and standardized in such a project structure system.

As for the setting of new items, the key is to find the most traditional elements mainly in the prototypes of traditional Yang style, Chen style and other boxing types, and ask for the opinions of folk boxers to build a standard technical system. In the new competition system, each action chosen by the athlete has value. However, in the past, many similar actions did not have value while the difficult action of skipping and jumping was of great value. This phenomenon will cease to exist in the future, which will make the tradition of martial arts inherited and carried forward.

Thirdly, there should be standards in Taijiquan competition. Culture needs to be expressed in symbols and specific behaviors. When the technique of Taijiquan competition has standards, culture will have a carrier. In recent years, many good jumping and balancing maneuvers with Olympic spirit have been designed in the development of competitive martial arts including Taijiquan's self-selected projects. There are no top scores for difficulty, and the score has exceeded 10 points for the highest difficulty. In some Olympic events, after some rotating difficulty moves, the two feet are used when landing, and for body shaking there is no deduced points. But in Taijiquan competitions, many difficult actions require one foot to land. One will be reduced points if there is sway when landing. Nowadays, there is a larger audience for Taijiquan competitions, because they can understand the Taijiquan competition and interact with the players properly. Therefore, the requirements for Taijiquan competition are higher and the overall performance of the sport is softer and slower. This combination of softness and hardness can help the audience appreciate its charm from their applause.

Fourthly, the movements of Taijiquan should be digitized by motion coding. The movements of Taijiquan are very complicated. Moreover many movements have image names. To standardlize it, it is necessary to set the digital technical code for all the movements. In the Olympics, only the diving project has this code. If we can do this job well, players in any country can use numbers to describe his movements, and the computer can directly identify the player's movements. This will make Taijiquan closely related to modern information technology, and the

三是竞赛技术有标准。文化要有符号来表达，要有具体的行为来表达，而当太极拳竞赛的技术有了标准，文化就有了载体。近年来，在竞技武术包括太极拳的自选项目发展中，设计了很多好的、具有奥运精神的跳跃动作、平衡动作。它们的难度不封顶，最高难度起评分已经突破10分。在一些奥运项目中，有些旋转难度动作后，落地时是采用双脚方式，身体晃动并不扣分，而太极拳比赛中，很多难度动作后要求单脚落地，落地时晃一点都要被扣分。现在太极拳比赛的观众越来越多，而且观众能够看懂太极拳比赛，能够与选手进行恰当的互动，所以太极拳比赛里动作标准更高，而整个运动外表表现又更柔、更缓，这种柔弱和刚强结合的动作，可以从观众的掌声中体现出它的魅力。

四是动作编码数字化。太极拳的动作非常复杂，很多动作都有非常形象的名称，要想将其标准化，就要将所有的动作都进行动作数字技术编码，而在奥运会中，也只有跳水项目才有这种编码。做好这项工作，任何国家的选手都可以用数字来描述他的动作，计算机可直接对选手动作进行识别。这样也就使太极拳与现代信息技术密切相关，使比赛由数字化技术控制，是一项具有创新意义的时代性变革。同时，对动作的技术要求也明确量化，这种量化要求不但诠释了太极拳内在的悬移运动本质，而且为它的健身功能和防止大众锻炼时的膝盖疼痛创造了很好的尺度。

五是运动员空间更大。在新的规则体系中，如果运动员十五六岁开始出成绩，那么30岁以前都可以练自选项目；而进入30岁以后，一些难度大的动作做不了了，仍可以接着打规定项目，这样将使运动员的运动寿命大大延长。

世界太极拳锦标赛的规则是两部。除了现有的套路外，随着逐步掌握了太极拳动作的功法和本质之后，中外运动员经过练习，不仅个人可以"演"武，还将进行"比"武。对于更多的运动员来说，随着

competition will be controlled by digital technology. It is an innovative change with the times. At the same time, the technical requirements for the movement are also clearly quantified. This quantitative requirement not only explains the inherent nature of the shift movements of Taijiquan, but also creates a good scale for its fitness function and prevention of knee pain during mass exercise.

Fifthly, the athletes have more space in sports life. In the new rules system, if the athletes start to perform excellently at the age of 15 or 16, they can continue to practice self-selected items until they are 30 years old. After the age of 30, they cannot do some difficult movements, but they can still play the prescribed items, which will greatly extend the athlete's sports life.

There are two rules for World Taijiquan Championship. In addition to the existing routines, if the Chinese and foreign athletes gradually master the practice essence of Taijiquan movements, they can not only perform but also compete with each other. Athletes are the backbone of the promotion of Taijiquan in the future, especially if the International Wushu Federation provides Taijiquan with an international standardization social popularization project through the ranking and examination system. And these will promote a virtuous circle of standardization systems in many aspects such as the qualification of the International Wushu Federation and the spread of Taijiquan.

In the folk heritage, it is necessary to integrate Chinese culture into the practice of Taijiquan transmission, set up a Taijiquan cultural brand, integrate the media network of transmission, establish a cooperation mechanism between official organizations and civil organizations, and expand the scope of the system. More importantly, how to promote Taijiquan and use its inherent health and fitness functions to improve human health and quality of life is the most central issue of the international community as well as the charm ot Taijiquan's inheritance and development.

Nowadays, human beings around the world face four major problems: First, the ageing of the global population is one of the greatest challenges in the 21st century. 1999 is the International Year of Older Persons, and the World Health Organization (WHO) has established its theme as "Active Ageing Makes the Difference". The proportion of chronic non-communicable diseases will continue to increase due to the extension of human life and lifestyle changes.

未来国际武联通过段位、考级制度把太极拳作为国际的标准化社会普及项目,他们就是将来太极拳推广普及的骨干、教练。而这些都将促进太极拳竞技比赛在国际武联的资格认证、太极拳传播等诸多环节中形成良性循环的标准化体系。

太极拳发源地——中国河南省温县陈家沟太极拳家庭式传承
Teaching Taijiquan at Home in Chenjiagou

在民间传承上,则需要将中国文化融入太极拳传播实践中,树立太极拳文化品牌,整合传播的媒介网络,建立官方组织与民间组织的合作机制,扩大段位制的范围等。更重要的是如何推广太极拳,利用其内在的养生健身功能,提高人类的健康水平和生活质量,这是国际社会最为关注的问题,也是太极拳在国际间传承发展的魅力所在。

现在全球人类面临四类大难题:一是全球人口的老龄化是21世纪人类面临的最大挑战之一。1999年是国际老年人年,世界卫生组织确定其主题为"积极健康的老年生活"。由于人类寿命的延长和生活方式的改变,慢性非传染疾病的比例将继续提高。心脑血管疾病、癌症、糖

Cardiovascular and cerebrovascular diseases, cancer, diabetes, dementia and osteoporosis will be the leading cause of death for older persons. Fractures are the most common complication of senile osteoporosis, especially in older women. Cerebrovascular diseases, Alzheimer's disease, and osteoporosis have become the main cause of the inability to take care of themselves for the elderly. The ageing of the population in the 21st century has created a major burden on society. How to improve the health and quality of life of the elderly and minimize the burden on families and society is a social issue that must be addressed and dealt with strategically. Secondly, adults are facing physical and mental health problems in a fiercely competitive environment. People's life rhythm is accelerated in modnern society and they have been in a fiece competition for a long time. Therefore the effective modes of exercise can help them maintain sufficient energy, improve work efficiency, enhance psychological endurance and delay ageing process, which is a topic of great strategic importance. Thirdly, the enhancement of the physical fitness of young people has received much attention from the society. Research proves that the development of the right brain is an important part of the comprehensive development of intelligence and physical fitness. It will not only fully develop the ingenuity of young people, but also lay a good foundation for the comprehensive improvement of young people's physical fitness. The development of adolescents' right brain potential and comprehensive improvement of physical fitness through appropriate methods and approaches has become an important topic for adolescent education. Fourthly, the high-tech of the society puts unprecedented demands on the ability and level of mental workers. It is a strategic issue to effectively improve people's intelligence and the ability of the human nervous system to work continuously and efficiently.

Years of practice and research results show that Taijiquan, as a traditional fitness treasure, can play its unique role in solving the above-mentioned problems, and can have a significant and even unexpected effect.

Taijiquan has the special effect of strengthening the body. First, Taijiquan has a great role in fully mobilizing people's spiritual initiative. It requires being loose and comfortable, body coordination, smooth blood, yin and yang balance, guiding moves by intention and the meridians, moving of *qi* through the whole body, and the unity between spirit and form. It grasps the human body state during

尿病，以及折磨老人的阿尔茨海默病、骨质疏松症将成为老年人死亡的主要原因。骨折是老年骨质疏松症最常见的并发症，尤以高龄女性最为显著。脑血管疾病、阿尔茨海默病、骨质疏松症成为老年人生活不能自理的主要病因。21世纪人口的老龄化，形成社会的重大负担。如何提高老年人的健康水平和生活质量，最大限度地减轻家庭和社会的负担，是必须提到战略高度来对待和处理的社会问题。二是处在激烈竞争环境中的成年人的身心健康问题。现代社会中人们生活节奏加快，长期处于激烈的竞争状态之中。因此，寻求有效的锻炼模式，使成年人保持充沛的精力、提高工作效率、提高心理承受力、延缓推迟他们的衰老进程，是一项具有重大战略意义的课题。三是全面增强青少年的体质备受社会关注。研究证明，开发右脑是使智力、体质全面发展的重要环节。它不仅能充分开发青少年的聪明才智，也将为青少年体质全面提升打下良好的基础。采用合适的方法和途径开发青少年的右脑潜能，全面增强体质，成为青少年教育科学的战略性的重要课题。四是社会的高科技化对脑力劳动者的能力和水平提出了前所未有的要求。如何有效地提高人们的智力，增强人类神经系统持续、高效工作的能力，是一项具有重大战略意义的课题。

多年的实践和研究结果表明，祖国传统健身瑰宝太极拳对于解决上述问题可以发挥其独特的作用，起到显著的甚至是意想不到的效果。

太极拳具有强身健体的特殊功效：一是太极拳具有充分调动人的精神能动性的巨大作用。太极拳讲究松静安舒，周身协调，通畅气血，阴阳平衡，以意领行，导引经络，气贯全身，神形合一；它从整体上把握人体状态的锻炼调整，对神经系统和内脏器官状态的调整具有特效。二是太极拳讲究柔顺，刚柔相济，随机转化，舍己从人，以柔克刚，利于人们的心态、心理的调整，发挥正面性格，减少负面情绪影响，增进人们的身心健康。三是太极拳讲究松静自然，对于解除精神紧张，提高精神对环境的适应能力具有特殊的功效。四是太极拳讲究保持舒畅的腹式

the whole exercise, and has a special effect to the nervous system and the internal organs. Second, Taijiquan requires suppleness and balance between hardness and softness, which facilitate people's mental and psychological adjustment. Besides, the practice can help establish a positive personality, reduce the influence of introverted personality, and enhance people's physical and mental health. Third, Taijiquan requires looseness and naturalness. It has a special effect on relieving mental stress and improving the ability of the spirit to adapt to the environment. Fourth, Taijiquan requires maintaining a comfortable abdominal deep breathing, thus promoting the visceral peristalsis, and regulating the internal organs and improving the function. People who are engaged in Taijiquan exercise generally feel that it has the special effect of strengthening the body.

Over the years, quantitative tests on electrocardio, electroencephalogram and blood lipid levels in the middle-aged and elderly populations have shown that Taijiquan provides a certain degree of improvement in heart and brain function. In people who have practiced Taijiquan for a long time, the a wave in the brainwaves of people occupies a dominant position, the main peak is prominent, the wave frequency is synchronized and ordered, and the brain function enters a good awakening state. From a modern medical point of view, this state can greatly enhance the body's internal organs and immunity. The results also show that Taijiquan can improve the mood, sleep, personality, memory and movement stability of the elderly, promote the improvement of heart function and metabolic function, and have significant anti-ageing effects. The microcirculation test results show that Taijiquan exercise can improve the microcirculation state of the human body.

Thanks to the distinctive advantages, Taijiquan has been so much popularized across the world that it has attracted and fascinated lots of people ranging from ordinary people to presidents.

Ho Chi Minh, the former chairman of the Labor Party of Vietnam and the founding father of the Democratic Republic of Vietnam, began to love Taijiquan in October 1956, when Zhou Enlai, the former premier of China and He Long, the former vice premier of China visited the neighboring country. During the visit, He Long made a detailed introduction to the values of Taijiquan in terms of health care. Ho was greatly interested and expressed the idea that he wanted to

深呼吸，可以促进内脏的蠕动，起到调整内脏、提高功能的作用。从事太极拳锻炼的人群普遍能感受到它具有强身健体的特殊功效。

多年来，对中老年人群的心电、脑电及血脂水平的定量测试结果表明，太极拳锻炼对心脑功能状态有一定程度的改善，长期练太极拳的人的脑电波中a波（觉醒波）占明显主导地位，主峰突出，波频率同步化、有序化，大脑机能进入良好的觉醒状态。从现代医学的观点看，这种状态能极大地增强人体内脏功能及免疫能力。研究结果还表明，太极拳能改善老年人的情绪、睡眠、性格、记忆力与动作稳定性，促进心脏功能、代谢功能的提高，有显著的抗衰老效果。对人群的微循环测试结果显示，太极拳锻炼能使人体微循环状态得到改善。

太极拳所具备的特殊作用使其得以在全世界广泛传播，并得到了人类的共同喜爱，上至一国总统，下至平民百姓，无不被太极拳的魅力折服。

胡志明，曾担任越南劳动党主席、越南民主共和国主席和政府总理，是现代越南国父。1956年10月中国总理周恩来与副总理贺龙访问越南时，贺龙向越南胡志明主席介绍了中国太极拳在医疗、保健方面的价值。胡志明希望中国能派员去教。于是，国家体委就派出了太极拳名家顾留馨去越南教胡志明练太极拳。

吉米·卡特，1977年任美国第39任总统。卡特在担任美国总统期间，中美两国正式建立了外交关系。卡特总统支持在美国介绍和传授太极拳，倡导以打太极拳来增强体质，而且还通过有关财政部门给予专项资金支持。卡特卸任以后，特别钟情太极拳，不但自己积极练习，还和夫人一起习练太极拳。

保罗·比亚是喀麦隆第二任总统，曾于1987年、1993年和2003年三次正式访华，并于2006年来华出席中非合作论坛北京峰会，2011年7月对中国进行国事访问。保罗·比亚70多岁时对中国太极拳的健身保健作用情有独钟，专门邀请中国太极拳师到总统府授拳。

learn Taijiquan. Later, the National Sports Commission of China sent Gu Liuxin, one of the famous Taijiquan masters at that time, to teach Ho the art in Vietnam.

Jimmy Carter, who became the 39th US president in 1977, also loved Taijiquan very much. Soon after the Sino-US diplomatic relation was formally established during his presidency, he strongly supported the teaching and learning of Taijiquan in America and advocated building up health through the art. He also asked the financial department to assign a special fund to promote the popularization of Taijiquan. After his retirement, he became more active in Taijiquan practice, and even did it together with his wife.

Paul Biya, the second president of Cameroon, began to be fascinated by the health care function of Taijiquan in his seventies. He had specially invited Chinese masters to his presidential palace to teach Taijiquan. He once paid state visits to China in 1987, 1993, 2003 and 2011, and attended the Beijing Summit of the Forum on China-Africa Cooperation in 2006.

In 2001, Vaclav Havel, the then-president of Czech, met Chen Xiaowang, a descendant of Taijiquan from China, and expressed his desire to learn the art.

In September 2005, the Crown Princess Victoria of the Kingdom of Sweden visited Ritan Park in Beijing and learned Taijiquan in the park.

In 2008, Latvian Prime Minister Ivars Godmanis learned to practice Taijiquan.

Michael Higgins was elected the ninth president of Ireland on October 29, 2011 and re-elected on October 26, 2018. On December 12, 2015, Higgins visited the headquarters of Alibaba in Hangzhou, China. In the corporation's office building, he was greatly impressed by a wonderful Taijiquan performance by Jack Ma's staff.

Charles Philip Arthur George Mountbatten-Windsor is the current Crown Prince of the UK. When he visited a veterans physiotherapy center in 2010, he showed great interest in Taijiquan and tried to learn a few basic postures. At that time, Prince Charles, 61, took a Taijiquan lesson during which two basic postures were taught by a trainer there. He raised his right arm above his head, twisted his right hand, and then repeated the process with his left arm and left hand. Prince Charles practiced intently, and could not help laughing for his awkward movements.

2001年，捷克总统瓦茨拉夫·哈维尔接见了来自中国的太极拳传人陈小旺，并向他表达了学习太极拳的愿望。

2005年9月，在北京访问的瑞典王国王储维多利亚公主来到北京日坛公园参观并在公园学练太极拳。

2008年，拉脱维亚总理伊万斯·戈德马尼斯学打太极拳。

迈克尔·希金斯于2011年10月29日当选爱尔兰第九任总统，2018年10月26日，再次当选总统。2015年12月12日，希金斯造访中国杭州阿里巴巴总部。在阿里的办公楼内，马云的团队为希金斯奉献了精彩的太极拳表演，希金斯总统非常喜欢。

查尔斯·菲利普·亚瑟·乔治·蒙巴顿－温莎是现任英国王储，他在2010年参观一处退伍士兵理疗中心时，对中国的太极拳产生了极大兴趣，并尝试着学习了几个招式。当年61岁的查尔斯王子在那里上了一节太极拳课，私人教练教授了他两个最基本的动作——先将右臂举过头顶，同时扭动右手，然后用左臂和左手重复这个过程。查尔斯王子一面聚精会神地练习，一面为自己不标准的动作而忍俊不禁。

2016年9月2日，正在上海对中国进行首次正式访问的加拿大总理贾斯廷·特鲁多，出席了上海中宏保险新品发布会。发布会期间，贾斯廷·特鲁多与中宏高管一起打起了太极拳，以鼓励消费者投入健康积极的生活方式。

2010年9月15日，应斐济政府邀请，由斐济青年体育部主办、中国武术协会承办，为期三个月的中国太极拳培训班，在斐济首都苏瓦市中心苏库娜公园举行了隆重的教程开班仪式。斐济总理姆拜尼马拉马在仪式上正式宣布中国太极拳培训教程启动，斐济青年体育部长博列、中国驻斐济使馆参赞费明星等发表热情洋溢的讲话，多位内阁部长、常秘等高级官员及斐济公务员代表和公众近百人共同见证了开班仪式，来自斐济公务员队伍的60多名学员参加了太极拳教程首次授课。

贝拉克·侯赛因·奥巴马是美国第44任总统，也是太极拳的粉

On September 2, 2016, Canadian Prime Minister Justin Trudeau, who was making his first official visit to China, attended a new product launching ceremony sponsored by Manulife-Sinochem Life Insurance Co., Ltd. in Shanghai. At the ceremony, Trudeau and the executives of this company showed a performance of Taijiquan to encourage consumers to engage in a healthy and active lifestyle.

On September 15, 2010, the launching ceremony of a three-month Chinese Taijiquan training course was held in the Sukhana Park in the center of Suva, the capital of Fiji. The course, sponsored by Fiji Ministry of Youth and Sports, was organized by Chinese Wushu Association at the invitation of the Fiji government. At the ceremony, Prime Minister Josaia Voreque Bainimarama officially announced the beginning of the course. Felipe Bole, Minister of Youth and Sports of Fiji, and Fei Mingxing, counselor of Chinese Embassy in Fiji, delivered passionate speeches respectively. Nearly 100 people, including several cabinet ministers and senior officials, some other Fijian civil servants and civilians, participated in the ceremony. And more than 60 Fiji civil servants attended the first class.

Barack Hussein Obama, the 44th president of the United States, is also fond of Taijiquan. In his address to the U.S. House of Representatives in 2009, Obama, for the first time, defined Taijiquan originated in China as the perfect aerobic exercise in the world. He advocated that American citizens should vigorously learn and promote the art. And Michelle Obama, the then-first-lady of the US, invited by her Chinese counterpart Peng Liyuan, visited China with her family members from March 20-26, 2014. On the morning of March 25, she went to No. 7 Middle School of Chengdu to learn Taijiquan. In this event, she experienced the unique charm of this traditional Chinese culture.

In order to further promote Taijiquan, the combination of inheritance and innovation should be adopted. Based on an in-depth understanding of the inner characteristics of Taijiquan, we should carry out Taijiquan routines that are relatively simple and easy to learn and have obvious special fitness functions. Under the cooperation of scientific experiments, Taijiquan not only absorbs the essence of classical boxing, but also develops according to the medical requirements of different diseases, creating a new routine that people like to

丝。2009年，奥巴马在美国众议院国会咨文上，第一次将发源于中国的太极拳运动定义为世界上最完美的有氧运动，并倡导美国社会和公民大力学习和推广太极拳。2014年3月20日至26日，应中国国家主席习近平夫人彭丽媛邀请，奥巴马夫人米歇尔及家人访华。25日上午，米歇尔来到成都第七中学身体力行地学起了太极拳，亲身体验中国传统文化的独特魅力。

为了太极拳的进一步传承推广，还应注重继承和创新相结合。在深入理解太极拳内在特点的基础上，发展相对简单易学、具有明显专项健身功能的太极拳套路。在科学实验的配合下，太极拳不仅吸取古典拳种的精华，还将根据不同病症的医学要求，创新发展，创编出人们喜闻乐见的新套路。

同时，太极拳理、拳论从经典理论向现代语言和现代科技诠释的过渡，也将推动太极拳运动的更大普及和向世界传播。将古老的东方文明与现代科技相结合，应用现代科技手段和理论方法来弘扬祖国传统文化，继承与创新相结合，必将加速探索太极拳优化生命质量奥秘的进程。在可以预见的将来，系统的太极拳锻炼，可能成为促进人们聪明智慧、身强力壮、精力充沛、延缓衰老、益寿延年的一个重要手段，为缓解21世纪社会的人口老龄化压力、提高中年人健康水平、开发青少年智力、提高脑力劳动能力，全面提高21世纪人类的健康水平和精神文明做出独特的贡献。

practice.

At the same time, the transition from classical theory to modern language, modern science and technology will also promote the popularity and spread of Taijiquan to the world. It will accelerate the process of exploring Taijiquan by combining ancient Eastern civilization with modern science and technology and applying modern science and technology methods to promote the traditional culture. In the foreseeable future, systematic practice of Taijiquan may become an important method to promote people's intelligence, strength, energy and longevity. It will also help to make a unique contribution to relieving the pressure on the ageing, the health of improvement of the middle-aged, the intelligence development of the young, the improvement of the labour ability, and the comprehensive improvement of human health and cultural progress in the 21st century.

第六章

# 太极拳名家的故事

---

Chapter Ⅵ

Stories of Well-known Taijiquan Masters

## 一、陈王廷校场比武

太极拳,想必大家都知道。但是要说太极拳的创始人,可能就有人不知道了,说不定还会牵扯出个来无影、去无踪的神仙人物,说什么夜梦玄武大帝秘授拳法,一夜间就变成了太极拳大仙。这些呢,都是一些攀仙附道糊弄人的天方奇谭,也叫说瞎话。真正的太极拳创始人呢,是明末清初的河南温县陈家沟人陈王廷。

陈王廷,出生于明朝万历二十八年,也就是公元1600年,清康熙十九年(1680)去世,享年八十岁高龄。

陈王廷出身于小官宦家庭,祖父和父亲均为明朝下级官吏。陈王廷自幼受到的教育就是传统的耕读传家,报效朝廷。到了崇祯末年,各地农民纷纷起义,大明江山社稷风雨飘摇,崇祯皇帝感到了前所未有的压力,急忙开了武科考,为国家选取忠勇义士。陈王廷本来就在朝思暮想如何报效朝廷,就去参加了那次乡试,要考武举。

陈王廷校场比武
Chen Wangting Competing in Military Skills at a Drill Ground

武科考分为武考与文考两步,武考分马上和马下,其中一项是跑马射箭。在十五步外设立靶垛,一马三箭,三马九箭,中四箭者为

# Ⅰ. Chen Wangting Competing in Military Skills at a Drill Ground

Taijiquan is probably known to all. But when it comes to the founder of Taijiquan, some people may not know about him. Maybe some will think of an immortal figure, who became a Taijiquan immortal overnight with the night dream of God Xuanwu secretly teaching him boxing. Actually, these are all fantastic fantasies, or lies. The real founder of Taijiquan is Chen Wangting, a native of Chenjiagou, Wenxian County, Henan Province, in the late Ming and early Qing period.

Chen Wangting was born in the 28th year of the Wanli Period in the Ming dynasty (1600 A.D.) and died at the age of eighty in the 19th year of the Qing dynasty (1680 A.D.).

It is said that Chen Wangting was born in the family of a petty governmental official. Both his father and grandfather were low-ranking officials of the Ming government. Chen Wangting was educated from his childhood as a traditional heir in farming and reading to serve the imperial court. At the end of Emperor Chongzhen's reign, peasants across the country rose up one after another, threatening the rule of the Ming government. The emperor felt unprecedented pressure and rushed to hold the military examination to select loyal and brave volunteers for the country. As Chen Wangting had been thinking to serve the imperial court every day, he went to take the provincial exam for the title of the martial arts.

The military examination was divided into two steps: the martial arts and the liberal arts. The martial arts test was composed of the infantry and horseback events, one of which was archery on a racing horse. The target stack is fifteen steps away. A contestant would shoot three arrows once on a racing horse, for a total of nine shots. The one who can hit the target four times is qualified into the next event. Chen Wangting practiced martial arts from an early age and was skilled in archery. So he actually hit the center of the target with all the nine arrows, like a bird rushing to occupy another's nest. On seeing this, the examiner was delighted, thinking that he had found another talent for the court. However, when the examiner was happy, he heard only three beats by the drummer who was in charge

合格，进入下一个环节。陈王廷自幼习武，箭法精湛，居然射出了后箭追前箭的凤夺巢，九箭九中，箭箭命中靶心。考官看得那是清清楚楚，乐得合不拢嘴，心想自己又为朝廷发现了栋梁之材。可是，考官正高兴的时候，却听到负责报靶的鼓吏咚、咚、咚擂了三通鼓，往后再没声响。三通鼓就是中三箭的意思，也就是说陈王廷落考了。

咳！这个下九流的鳖家也敢来欺负你陈爷爷，吃我一刀！陈王廷年轻气盛，心中不服，催马向前，手起刀落，报靶鼓吏的脑袋立即搬了家。

然后，陈王廷一身正气，来到主考官面前，施礼完毕，说："启禀主考大人，学生杀了一只鳖。"

"扔到河里算啦！"

陈王廷忠实厚道，压根没有想到主考官因为爱惜人才暗里在替自己开脱罪责，反而以为主考大人没有听清，继续说道："大人，我杀的是一只人鳖！"

主考大人见陈王廷不知避祸，开脱不成了，只好公事公办，严厉喝道："杀人者，偿命！"

陈王廷这下听明白了，大惊失色，知道自己闯下的是滔天大祸，急忙拨马冲出考场，逃难而去。

## 二、陈王廷防守黄河

话说陈王廷策马冲出开封校场，直奔登封御寨山好汉李际遇处避难。这一避就是三年！当时，朝廷有一个规定，凡是犯了大罪的人，只要逃难三年不被官府逮住，就不再追究了。陈王廷在山寨度日如年，好不容易熬够了三年的时间，思乡之心日益迫切，李际遇也看出了陈王廷的心思，就暗中派遣手下将领蒋发前往怀庆府温县陈家沟去探听虚实。

of the target reporting. No more beats followed. Three beats means hitting the target with three arrows. That is to say, Chen Wangting failed the exam.

"Hey! How dare you bastard bully me! I'll kill you!" Chen Wangting, young and vigorous, refused to accept the result. He urged the horse to move forward, raising his hand and dropping his broadsword. Then the head of the drummer was removed immediately.

Then, Chen Wangting came to salute the examiner with all his integrity, reporting, "I killed a turtle."

"Throw it away into the river!"

Chen Wangting was faithful and honest. He did not realize that the examiner was secretly excusing himself for his talent. Instead, he thought that the examiner had not heard him clearly. He went on to say, "Sir, I killed a bastard instead of a turtle!"

When the examiner saw that Chen Wangting did not know how to avoid a misfortune, he had to do business and drastically shouted, "Killers must pay for their lives!"

Chen Wangting then understood what happened and was shocked that he was in a terrible disaster. He rushed on horse out of the examination field and fled.

## II. Chen Wangting Guarding along the Yellow River

Chen Wangting rushed out of the drill ground in Kaifeng and went straight to take refuge from Li Jiyu, a hero in the Yuzhai Mountain in Dengfeng. This refuge lasted for three years. At that time, there was a rule in the court that whoever committed a major crime, as long as he fled for three years and was not caught by the government, he would not be prosecuted any longer. Chen Wangting spent his days with deep worries in the fortified mountain village. After three years, his homesickness was becoming more and more serious. Li Jiyu also saw what Chen Wangting was worried about and secretly sent his general Jiang Fa to Chenjiagou, Wenxian County, Huaiqing Prefecture, to explore if Chen Wangting was still being hunted.

After Jiang Fa took command, he went straight to Chenjiagou. Upon

蒋发领命之后，径直前往陈家沟。到了村里一打听，方知三年来从无官府来陈家沟寻找陈王廷。为什么会这样呢？此处暗表：这一是因为各地狼烟四起，农民起义不断；二是因为主考大人同情陈王廷，怜惜其出众武功，压根就没将陈王廷校场过失杀人的事情向上通报。

蒋发回到登封，将陈家沟的情况向李际遇做了报告。李际遇将此情一直隐瞒了很长时间，他怕陈王廷得知实情后离开山寨。后来，见陈王廷追问得紧迫，李际遇才不得不将实情相告。

陈王廷坚守黄河防务
Chen Wangting Guarding along the Yellow River

原来如此！看来我还可以报效朝廷啊！陈王廷得知官府根本就没派人追拿自己，心中感激之余，更是喜出望外，当即打点行李，连夜下山，直奔家乡温县陈家沟。

这个时候，朱明王朝气数将尽，各地造反，朝廷那是应接不暇。陈王廷回到陈家沟时，正值河南土寇猖獗之时，因为他武艺出众，很

inquiry in the village, he learnt that no officers from the government had been to Chenjiagou for three years searching for Chen Wangting. Why? Here's the reason revealed secretly: this is partly because peasant uprisings arose across the country and partly because the examiner never reported Chen Wangting's accidental killing at the drill ground because of his sympathy for Chen Wangting and pitying Chen's outstanding martial arts.

Jiang returned to Dengfeng and reported the situation of Chenjiagou to Li Jiyu. Li Jiyu kept this secret for a long time because he was afraid that Chen Wangting would leave the mountain village after he learned the truth. Later, when Chen Wangting asked him urgently, Li Jiyu had to tell the truth.

"I see! It seems that I can still serve the court!" Chen Wangting was overjoyed to learn that the government had not sent anyone to arrest him. He was grateful and immediately packed up his luggage and went down the mountain overnight to his hometown, Chenjiagou, Wenxian County.

At this time, the ruling of the Ming dynasty was close to an end as rebellions were so widespread that the court was overwhelmed. When returning to Chenjiagou, Chen Wangting, with his outstanding martial arts, soon caught the attention of Wu Conghui, the county commander of Henan Province. Wu Conghui, a man good at valuing talents with courtesy, visited Chen Wangting in Chenjiagou and asked him to serve as a commander of the countryside forces. Chen Wangting was pleased to accept the invitation of the magistrate and took up his post. He joined Guo Zhong, the chief commander, in guarding the Yellow River and defending against local invaders.

Wu Conghui, a native of Anping County, Jinzhou, Zhending Prefecture, Hebei Province, was appointed assistant prefectural magistrate of Huaiqing Prefecture and the official in charge of Wenxian affairs. Rioters went straight up the Yellow River from east to west until they reached the town of Wenxian County. Wu Conghui led the local soldiers and the government guards to fight against those ferocious rioters and aggressors. The county town was in danger of being seized.

When Chen took office, he inspected the defense of the town on the spot and found that rioters and bandits were overwhelming the town by collecting a large number of wooden boats and sailing against the water to besiege the town

快就引起了县令吴从诲的注意。吴从诲礼贤下士，亲自到陈家沟拜访陈王廷，请其出任乡兵守备。陈王廷乐得个恭敬不如从命，接受了吴县令的拜请，走马上任，与千总郭忠一起，守黄河，防土寇。

吴从诲，河北真定府晋州安平县人，举人出身，任怀庆府通判并署温县事。贼寇自东而西，沿河直上，直到温县县城城下。吴从诲率领乡兵与官府守兵拼死抵抗，奈何贼寇势大，温县县城岌岌可危。

陈王廷到任后，实地察看城池防务，发现贼寇势众，还征集了大批木船，逆水行舟围困温县，企图攻取。一直胸怀报国之心的陈王廷熟读兵书，胸有成竹，就向县令吴从诲提出：用火攻，退贼寇。

吴从诲听从了陈王廷的建议，命令官兵千总郭忠与乡兵守备陈王廷调度兵马，准备硫磺、芒硝、柴草、火把一应用物，趁着夜黑风高，放火直烧贼船。

郭忠与陈王廷做了分工，守备陈王廷率乡兵放火烧船，千总郭忠率官兵掩杀土寇。

陈王廷率乡兵乘小船前往贼营放火，黄河上火焰滔天，土寇被烧得哭爹叫娘，郭忠率官兵箭射、刀劈、枪刺，土寇纷纷跳河逃生。俗话说"黄河无底海无边"，由于不识水性，贼寇在河中被淹死者无数，匪首一看损兵折将，大势已去，急忙下令撤兵。匪兵侥幸逃命者，顺河逃窜。

郭忠立功心切，正要挥师追击。陈王廷连忙阻止，说："郭千总，穷寇勿追！"郭忠正战在兴头上，又哪里听得进陈王廷的忠告，心中嘲笑陈王廷胆儿小，带领官兵继续乘船追击。堪堪就要追上贼众，不料一个匪首模样的回头张弓，郭忠中箭，落水而亡。

## 三、陈王廷木门寨讨牛

当年登封御寨山好汉李际遇手下曾有几千号人马，其中有位号称

in an attempt to capture it. Chen Wangting, who always cherished serving the country, was familiar with military books and knew how to handle the situation. He advised Wu Conghui, the county magistrate, to attack the bandits with fire.

Wu Conghui followed Chen's suggestion and ordered the chief commander Guo Zhong and Chen Wangting to gather troops and horses, preparing sulfur, mirabilite, firewood and torches, to set fire to the bandits' boats during a dark night with a strong wind.

Guo Zhong and Chen Wangting made a division of labor. Chen Wangting was responsible for leading troops to set fire to the boats, and Guo Zhong, the chief officer, for killing the aggressors.

Chen Wangting led the local soldiers to set fire in a small boat to the bandits' camp. The flames on the Yellow River were so violent that the local aggressors were burned and cried for help. Guo Zhong led the officers and soldiers to shoot arrows at, cut and stab the enemy, and the local aggressors jumped into the river one after another to escape. As the saying goes, "The Yellow River has no bottom and the sea is boundless". Because they lacked the ability to swim, numerous bandits drowned in the river. As many soldiers and generals were lost, the bandit leaders hastily ordered the withdrawal of their troops. Some bandits escaped by chance and fled along the river.

Guo Zhong was earnestly dedicated and was about to pursue with his divisions. Chen Wangting quickly stopped Guo Zhong and said, "Commander Guo, don't chase the poor aggressors!" Guo Zhong, in high spirits of fighting, could not take Chen's advice, deriding Chen's timidity. He led the officers and soldiers to chase after them by boat. When he was about to catch up with the fleeing bandits, he was struck by an unexpected arrow shot by a bandit leader. Guo fell into the water and died.

## III. Chen Wangting Asking for the Lent Ox at Mumenzhai

At that time, Li Jiyu, a hero from the Yuzhai Mountain in Dengfeng, had thousands of men and horses under his command. Among them, there was a man named Jiang Fa, known as "the Fleet Footed". He and Chen Wangting formed a close friendship when Chen stayed in the mountain village. After Li Jiyu's defeat,

"飞毛腿"的叫蒋发。在山寨,他与陈王廷结下了深厚的情谊。李际遇兵败之后,蒋发投奔陈王廷,落户在陈家沟。

陈王廷出生于武术世家,惯使一把春秋大刀,胯下一匹枣红色战马,蓄有美髯,江湖上就将他比作三国时期的英雄关羽关云长,唤他"二关公"。"二关公"陈王廷走镖齐鲁一带,匪寇闻名丧胆,但也有不知天高地厚之辈,心中不服,前来寻衅滋事。

一天早上,陈王廷正在陈家沟的东沟中晨练,蒋发慌慌张张地跑了过来,递给陈王廷一张纸条。

陈王廷接过一看,只见上面写着四句话:家住山东木门寨,慕名陈沟来借牛。无缘对面不相逢,有缘处处皆朋友。

陈王廷看后哈哈大笑,对蒋发说:"江湖豪杰来访,有来无往非礼也,你陪我往山东木门寨走一遭吧!"

陈王廷与蒋发一道直奔山东,路遇一名自称途经木门寨的生意人同道做伴,晓行夜宿,不一日,来到了木门寨吊桥楼下。

只听寨内"咚"的一声号炮响,寨楼上呼啦啦拥出一彪人马,为首一位长者,苍髯红面气宇轩昂,向陈王廷拱手道:"王廷先生见请了!"

蒋发见寨主只说话,不落吊桥,不开寨门,心中正纳闷,却见陈王廷翻身下马,朝寨主一拱手,一只胳膊挟住了战马,另一手提起春秋大刀,一个旱地拔葱,早已越过寨壕,再一纵,眨眼间就登上了寨墙。

寨主上前与陈王廷见礼,下了寨墙,请陈王廷先行通过一条两三丈深的胡同。

陈王廷刚进胡同口落下脚,只见胡同里三支连珠箭嗖嗖嗖射出,陈王廷看得真切,伸手接住一支飞箭,拨落另外两支飞箭,施展轻功,疾步穿越胡同,此时暗道内的弩箭纷纷射出,将他身后墙上射得如同刺猬一般。

寨主见了暗暗佩服,又请陈王廷过第二道门。

Jiang Fa fled to Chen Wangting and settled in Chenjiagou.

Born in a family of martial artists, Chen Wangting used to use a long broadsword while riding a jujube-red horse. With a beautiful beard, he was compared to Guan Yu (whose courtesy name is Yunchang, famous for his loyalty and righteousness and was called Guan Gong later), the hero of the Three Kingdoms period. Therefore, he was called "Guan Gong the second". Chen Wangting earned a fearsome reputation while making trips to Shandong as a bodyguard, but there were also bandits who had an exaggerated opinion of themselves and came to challenge him.

One morning, while Chen Wangting was drilling at the east gully of Chenjiagou, Jiang Fa ran over in a panic, handing him a note.

Chen Wangting took a look at the note, which said, "I live in the Mumenzhai Village, Shandong Province, and I want to borrow an ox from Chenjiagou. If there is luck between us, we will become friends."

Chen Wangting laughed and said to Jiang Fa, "Friendship cannot stand always on one side. Let's go to Mumenzhai in Shandong Province."

Chen Wangting and Jiang Fa went straight to Shandong. On their way, they met a fellow businessman who claimed to pass by Mumenzhai. They traveled in the day and slept at night. Within a day, they came to the suspension bridge at Mumenzhai.

A sound of a gun signal from the village was followed by a crowd of people, who rushed out from the gate tower of the village. The leading one was an elder, with a grey beard and a red face, who looked energetic and impressive, and greeted Chen Wangting, "Mr. Chen Wangting, Welcome to my village!"

Jiang Fa was puzzled when the village chief only spoke but did not drop the suspension bridge to open the gate. Surprisingly, he saw Chen Wangting dismounted from his horse and made a gesture of greeting at the chief. Holding the horse in one hand and raising his long broadsword in the other, Chen jumped across the trench and climbed the wall in the blink of an eye.

The chief went to greet Chen Wangting and they went down the wall. He asked Chen Wangting to go through a ten-meter-long alley first.

As soon as Chen Wangting had just entered the alley entrance, three arrows flew from the inside one after another. He could see them clearly, catching one

这第二道门与第一个胡同相仿，只不过是将弩箭换成了梅花桩，用二三尺长的木桩，按梅花型排列，隐藏于墙壁之内，只要误踩机关，木桩便由墙内强力射出，二木相撞，可将人撞成肉泥烂酱。

陈王廷见多识广，早已看透了木门寨寨主的把戏，再次施展轻功，穿越而过，寨主的算计再次落空。

就这样，陈王廷在机关重重的木门寨中如履平地，木门寨寨主大为惊叹，几次比武也都输于陈王廷。最后，木门寨寨主与陈王廷开怀畅饮，义结金兰。

陈王廷与蒋发在木门寨被盛情款待，住了些时日，但一直不见寨主归还借走的牛，蒋发忍不住问寨主："寨主，这牛不会是有借无还吧？"寨主哈哈大笑道："那牛早已在陈家牛棚之中了！"

## 四、陈王廷闷来造拳

上回说到，陈王廷心中高兴，认为自己终于找到了报效朝廷的路子，正欲精忠报国之时，无奈明王朝气数已尽，朱姓江山摇摇欲坠。闯王李自成从陕西一路杀进了北京城，吴三桂英雄一怒为红颜，不堪爱妾陈圆圆受辱，勾结清兵入关，朱明朝廷就此覆灭，天下易主，清王朝很快占领中原，执掌了华夏江山。

留头不留发，留发不留头。明朝万历年间，中国人口已经将近两亿，经历了明末清初的朝代更迭，到了清初顺治年间，中国人口一下子下降至四五千万了，战争猛于虎，一多半的国人丧失了性命。

经历了这场历史大变革，目睹了多少亲友生离死别，陈王廷可以说是悲痛欲绝，经常在陈家沟南边的黄河滩中徘徊，不知该如何安排自己的人生之路。心中郁闷时，便操起家伙什儿练武，心情舒畅时，就读读经书，研研兵法。到后来，天下渐趋平定之时，陈王廷也带着蒋发，走出陈家沟，访访友，放松放松心情。后来他也想明白了，自

and pulling down the other two. Then he made light steps to cross the alley at a rapid pace, dodging an array of arrows shot from the underpass and leaving the wall behind him like a hedgehog.

Then the village chief admired Chen Wangting secretly and asked him to cross the second gate.

What was behind this gate was similar to the first alley, but the crossbow arrows were replaced with staggered wooden piles, two or three feet long, hidden in the wall and arranged according to the plum blossom pattern. As long as the trigger was trampled by mistake, the wooden piles would shot out forcefully from inside the wall. A passerby could be smashed by two colliding piles.

As Chen Wangting understood the tricks of the chief before entering the second gate, he once again performed his light steps and crossed the second gate. The chief's tricks failed again.

In this way, Chen Wangting broke through the different barriers set in the village as easy as walking on a flat land. The village chief was greatly amazed and he also lost several competitions with Chen Wangting. Finally, the village chief and Chen Wangting enjoyed a good drink and became sworn brothers.

Chen Wangting and Jiang Fa were treated at Mumenzhai for some days. As the village chief mentioned nothing about the borrowed cattle, Jiang Fa couldn't help asking the chief, "Chief, can't the ox be returned?" The village chief laughed heavily and said, "That ox has already been in the Chen's cowshed!"

## Ⅳ. Chen Wangting Creating Taijiquan

As mentioned above, Chen Wangting was happy that he had finally found a way to serve the court, only to find that the Ming dynasty under the Zhu's ruling was on the verge of collapse. The uprising leader Li Zicheng led his troops to occupy Beijing along the way from Shaanxi. Wu Sangui, a general of the Ming government, collaborated with the Qing army, leading to their swarming into the land of the Ming through the Shanhai Pass because he could not bear the fact that his beloved concubine Chen Yuanyuan had been insulted and humiliated. With the collapse of the Ming dynasty, the Manchu people soon occupied the Central Plains and the whole China at large.

以为拥兵百万、沃野万里的大明江山都能在顷刻间改弦易主,自己也就是一个满腔热血的武林好汉,既然回天乏力,不如种田看书习武,修身养性,怡养天年,尽享天伦之乐。

温县城西有一座千年古刹名叫慈胜寺,与洛阳白马寺隔着黄河遥相呼应。陈王廷在慈胜寺偶遇戚继光部将、高僧大德。交谈之中,他学到了更多的交战经验。自此,陈王廷经常前去拜访,学习戚家军武术,时间久了,与大德高僧结下情谊。大德高僧在坐化之际,亲手将一部书籍交予陈王廷,陈王廷万分感激,收下了这部抗倭名将戚继光著述的《纪效新书》,日夜研读,受益匪浅。

学习之后,方知自己学识浅薄,于是陈王廷又北上阳洛山,来到道教上清派创始人魏华存修道的二仙庙,拜访掌门道姑元弘,请教《黄庭经》炼神秘诀。元弘道姑深感陈王廷慈善恳诚,便将门内修炼法悉数传教,陈王廷感谢不已。

后来,陈王廷得知温县城神农涧有一位得道医家秦时月,立即登门拜访。秦时月也耳闻陈王廷名声,乐意结交,将自己掌握的中医经络病理与生死穴位要诀尽付陈王廷,并传授了导引、吐纳行功秘法。陈王廷与秦时月义结金兰,两人往来不绝,共同研究中医机理。

秦时月见陈王廷乐于研究阴阳之变,便将陈王廷引荐到自己的好友司马乾处。司马乾是易理行家,对五行八卦之理研究颇深,他的言论让陈王廷耳目一新,有醍醐灌顶、茅塞顿开之悟,从天地开辟到芸芸众生,对万事万物生发之理,都有了新的理解。陈王廷心境大开,好不兴奋。

闲暇时,陈王廷带着蒋发又遍访武林好友,切磋武艺,同时不断用新的理念来修正家传拳法,逐渐形成了一套阴阳相合、刚柔相济、以柔克刚、威力无比的新拳法。因为这套拳法秉承了太极阴阳变化之理,又吸收了诸家武术之长,陈王廷称之谓"太极拳",并且写下长短句《叙怀》警示后人。

Hair or head became a choice for the countrymen. During the Wanli period of the Ming dynasty, the Chinese population exceeded 200 million. But it suddenly dropped to 40 to 50 million by the Shunzhi period of the early Qing dynasty. The wars in late Ming and early Qing dynasties were fiercer than a tiger as they brought not only the dynastic change but also the loss of more than half of the population.

After this great historical change and witnessing the loss of many of his relatives and friends, Chen Wangting was so grieved that he often wandered along the Yellow River bank on the south of Chenjiagou, thinking over how to plan his future life. When he was depressed, he would practice martial arts. When he was in a good mood, he would read classics and study the art of war. Later, when the country became stable, Chen Wangting, together with Jiang Fa, went out of Chenjiagou to visit friends for relaxation. Later, he learned something from the fact that the Ming dynasty, even with millions of soldiers and a vast land, could be replaced by a new dynasty in a short period. In his mind, he himself was just a warm-blooded man of martial arts; since he could not change the political situation, why not cultivate his own mind to live happy days by farming, reading and practicing martial arts?

There was a thousand-year-old temple named the Cisheng Temple in the west of Wenxian, which echoed the White Horse Temple in Luoyang across the Yellow River. One day, Chen Wangting met Dade, a general under the then anti-Japanese strategist Qi Jiguang and a great monk, at the Cisheng Temple. During their conversation, Chen learned much more about warfare. Since then, he often paid visits to the general to learn the martial arts created by Qi Jiguang (1528-1588, a strategist of the Ming dynasty). As a result, he made a close friendship with the great monk. When the great monk died while sitting cross-legged, he handed over a book titled *New Treatise on Military Efficiency*, written by Qi Jiguang, to Chen Wangting. Chen was so grateful that he studied it day and night and benefited a lot.

After learning something, Chen Wangting was aware that he had a lot to explore. Then he went north to the Yangluo Mountain, to the Erxian Temple, where Wei Huacun, founder of the Taoist Upper Qing School, had cultivated herself. There he paid a visit to Yuanhong, the chief Taoist nun, to consult *Huang Ting Jing (The Yellow Court Classic)* for mysterious tricks. As Yuanhong was deeply impressed by his kindness and sincerity, she taught Chen all her cultivation

## 五、陈所乐平皋纵子

陈王廷门下有两位得意弟子，一个是陈所乐，一个是陈汝信。这两位高手是太极拳第二代宗师。

花开两朵，各表一枝。今天别的咱不说，只讲陈所乐。陈所乐生性豪爽，武艺高强，行侠仗义，深得乡亲们和武林同道的推崇。

陈所乐持家有方，家境富裕，又喜得双胞胎儿子陈恂如、陈申如，春风得意，好生快活。两个儿子从小跟随陈所乐习练太极拳，早早就成了太极高手。由于娇子心切，陈所乐对两个儿子宠爱有加。这小哥儿俩打从小起，从春末夏初就只穿个红兜肚上街，直到秋尽冬来。

这一天，陈家沟东边的平皋村有大集，陈所乐手里拎个长烟袋，带着一双七岁的宝贝儿子前去逛集买东西。

只见恂如、申如小哥儿俩头上留着一小撮系着红头绳的宝贝小辫儿，挂着红肚兜，小鸡鸡儿在裆下扑扑溜溜，跟着爹爹陈所乐前去赶集。六七岁的孩子，正是手不闲的年龄，一路蹦蹦跳跳，追逐嬉戏，爷儿仨尽享天伦，脸上都乐得像开了花。

平皋以前是座县城，现在是一个好几千人的大村，集市也是个大集，大街上生意摊儿一个挨一个，人头攒动，熙熙攘攘，好不热闹。恂如、申如一见人多，更是如鱼得水，在人群里挤来挤去，东跑西窜。

平皋村有一大户原家，家里人多，雇有长工、短工很多人。这天正好一名帮工外出挑水，在大街上经过，一不小心，桶里的水溅了出来，洒了恂如与申如一身。

帮工见是俩小孩，就不太在意了，也没想起道个歉，径直要走，恂如与申如不干了，俩人一把拽住了帮工，说："你的水洒我身上

methods, for which Chen was much grateful.

Later, when Chen Wangting learned that there was a Taoist physician named Qin Shiyue in Shennongjian, Wenxian, he immediately visited the doctor. Qin was pleased to make friends with Chen because of his reputation. He taught Chen Wangting about the key points of TCM meridian pathology, and the secret methods of *daoyin* and breathing. So they became sworn brothers and exchanged views constantly to study the mechanism of traditional Chinese medicine.

When Qin Shiyue found that Chen Wangting was happy to study the theory of yin and yang, he introduced Chen to his friend Sima Qian, an expert in the theory of change, who studied the theories of the Five Elements and the Eight Diagrams. Sima's remarks impressed Chen very much, enlightening him about the creation of all things from the beginning of the universe to all the living plants and animals. Chen was quite excited for his refreshing understanding of the world.

In his spare time, Chen Wangting, along with Jiang Fa, visited almost all the friends in the martial arts circle to discuss skills. At the same time, he constantly revised the traditional boxing method of his family with his acquired theories, and gradually formed a set of new boxing methods, which consisted of yin and yang, rigidity and softness, and flexibility and strength. As this set of boxing methods adhered to the principle of Taiji yin and yang, and absorbed the strengths of various martial arts, Chen Wangting called it Taijiquan, and wrote a poem titled "Narration of Ideas in Mind" to share with later generations.

## V. Chen Suole Spoiling His Sons in Pinggao

Chen Wangting took pride in his two disciples, Chen Suole and Chen Ruxin, who were the second generation masters of Taijiquan.

The two masters could be discussed separately. Today, we will talk about Chen Suole alone. He was bold, skilled and chivalry, winning the praise of fellow villagers and martial artists.

Chen Suole lived a decent life with his industriousness. In addition, his newly-born twin sons, Chen Xunru and Chen Shenru, added more happiness to his life. They followed Chen Suole to learn Taijiquan when they were quite young, and they soon became adept at Taijiquan. As Chen Suole doted on his sons, the

了，你不能走！"

帮工一看，不耐烦地说："小鳖孩子，快松手，不然招打了！"恂如与申如一听，更不愿意了，说："你这人这么大了，咋不知道讲理，还骂人！"帮工急了，放下水桶，去打恂如与申如，结果一个也没有打到，反而被俩小孩儿上下乱打一气，好不丢人。

帮工见自己打不过俩小孩儿，就招呼其他人帮忙。村里好事之人为讨好原家大户，纷纷上前帮忙，捉拿恂如、申如。恂如、申如熟知太极卸劲之法，以柔克刚，犹如泥鳅一般，虽说平皋原家帮忙的人多，却也捉拿不住，两个小孩子如入无人之境，窜蹦跳跃，玩得十分开心。

"咦，反了！反了！俩小孩子要蹚平平皋村了，这还了得！操家伙儿！"突然间，有人高声吆喝鼓动平皋村人操家伙什儿，准备大战恂如与申如。

这时，蹲在路边的陈所乐抽了一口烟，然后站起身，用烟袋锅儿拨打着一干平皋人，来到大街当中，说："这俩孩子是无家无主了，你们村人把水洒小孩子身上，连个歉也不道，还出口骂人，现在又想全村人上来打，这是不是有点欺人太甚了？再打，我可就不愿意了！"

众人一听，知道自己无理，纷纷低下了头。但也有不知死活的人，上前问："你是哪村的，敢来平皋村挑事？"陈所乐说："我是陈家沟陈所乐，俩小孩是我儿子！"众人一听，方知惹下大事儿来了。

## 六、太极天王双英破敌

话说陈恂如、陈申如从小闹过平皋村，弄得十里八村闻听陈家沟就不战而走，及至这对双胞胎长到十五六岁时，再一次大闹平皋村，更是威名远扬，武林人称"大天王""二天王"。

这是康熙年间的一个腊月，天空飘起了鹅毛大雪。一群从山西抢

twin boys went to the streets, with red abdomen wrappers alone, from late spring and early summer until the end of autumn.

One day, there was a large fair in Pinggao Village located to the east of Chenjiagou. Chen Suole took his seven-year-old twin sons to the fair for shopping, with a long stemmed tobacco pipe in hand.

Both Xunru and Shenru were wearing a small lovely pigtail bound with red strings on their heads and red abdomen wrappers, with their butts being bare. The children of six or seven years old were restless, chasing and playing all the way to the fair. The father and his sons all enjoyed their journey so much that they looked highly delighted.

Pinggao had been a county town, but now it was a village of thousands of residents. There was a big market, with various stalls being set up and crowed people on the street. Seeing there were a lot of men and women, Xunru and Shenru were excited enough to chase in the crowd, as if the fish had got into the water again.

There was a wealthy and influential family named Yuan in the village of Pinggao. As it was a big family, many long-term and short-term laborers were hired. On this day, a helper went out to carry water and passed through the street. Accidentally, the water in a bucket splashed out onto Xunru and Shenru.

When the laborer found that they were two children, he didn't care too much and went away immediately without apologizing to them. Xunru and Shenru were very angry, grabbing the man and saying, "You spilled water on us! You can't go!"

The worker said impatiently, "Damn, let go or take a beating!" On hearing this, Xunru and Shenru were much more in a rage. "As a grown-up, why are you so brutal to swear at us?" The man could not stand this and put down the bucket and went to hit the two boys. Instead of striking them, he was beaten up and down by the twins, which made him feel so disgraced.

Knowing that he could not overwhelm the two children, the man asked others to help him. Some men in the village, who were busy bodies to please the Yuan family, had come to capture the two boys. Xunru and Shenru were very joyful as they jumped like loaches in and out of those "helping" hands. However, many failed to catch the two boys as they were familiar with the Taiji method of unloading strength, overcoming hardness with softness.

劫回来的山东响马,来到了平皋村,直奔大户王家。王家在平皋村家大业大,为了防范盗匪,院子里布置有天罗地网,一般人难进难出,但响马人多,蜂拥而入。家主王遴为人乐施好善,忠诚厚道,见到这种阵仗,心里十分害怕,赶紧酒肉伺候,不敢得罪。

但是土匪响马入门,可并不是能够轻松打发走的,王遴的脸上不由露出为难之色,连连长吁短叹,不知如何是好。

王遴如此表情,引起了儿媳妇陈氏的注意。陈氏问道:"公爹,莫不是遇到了什么难事?"王遴叹了口气说:"家里招响马了,来了十好几个,祸事临门了。"

陈氏听了后说:"公爹,您让车把式给我备匹马,我回趟娘家。"

王遴知道亲家是太极拳高手,就连忙让车把式给儿媳备马。陈氏策马直奔陈家沟,去见父亲陈所乐。

陈所乐正在家中闲坐,见女儿骑马回家,大吃一惊,连忙问女儿出了什么事。女儿便前来后去地给父亲讲了一遍。陈所乐听完,笑了笑说:"闺女,你回去告诉你公爹,让他好酒好菜招待。只是今天晚饭要等到掌灯以后,一切我自有安排。"

陈氏回到平皋村,给公爹一五一十地做了交代,说明是娘家爹爹陈所乐的意思。王遴听后,心中多少有些坦然,急忙去做安排。

天将傍晚,陈所乐将双胞胎儿子喊了过来,说:"你们俩一会儿背半袋豌豆,带上家什,去你姐家把那伙响马收拾了!"

陈恂如、陈申如闻听大喜,他俩最喜欢干这事。俩人一路疾行来到平皋村姐姐家,直奔正堂而去。这哥儿俩对姐姐家的地形非常熟悉。到了正堂屋门口,见屋里明灯蜡烛,响马们吆五喝六,正在海吃痛饮。

申如手持腊木杆,低低地问:"哥,是你先进,还是我先进?"陈恂如顺手一推陈申如:"你进去吧,别啰唆了!"

扑扑通通,陈申如一头栽进了正堂屋,进得屋来,陈申如先用腊

"Oh! Out of control! Out of control! Two children are going to ruin the Pinggao Village. That's going too far! Get weapons!" Suddenly, someone shouted and encouraged the villagers to find weapons to fight against Xunru and Shenru.

At this time, Chen Suole, squatting on the side of the road, took a puff of cigarette, then stood up and struck a gang of Pinggao villagers with his cigarette bag. He came to the middle of the street and said, "Are these two children homeless? The villager sprinkled water on them and cursed them even without an apology. Now the whole villagers want to bully them. Isn't it going too far? If you don't stop, I won't stand this!"

Knowing that they were in the wrong, the villagers bowed their heads, keeping silent. But a man who did not distinguish good from bad went up and asked, "Where are you from? Dare to come to Pinggao to make trouble!" "I am Chen Suole from Chenjiagou. The two children are my sons!" said Chen Suole. Then, everyone knew that they had got in big trouble.

## VI.  Twin Brothers Capturing Bandits

There were once twin brothers in Chengjiagou Village, Chen Xunru and Chen Shenru, whose win in the fight against bandits in the Pinggao Village when they were very young would scare away many bandits in the neighbouring area. When they were fifteen or sixteen years old, their second fight in Pinggao made them more well-known. They were also praised as "the elder hero" and "the younger hero" by people in the *wushu* circle.

It was one day in December of the Chinese lunar calendar during the reign of Emperor Kangxi in the Qing dynasty, when it was snowing heavily. A group of bandits came to Pinggao Village, and broke into the house owned by a rich man named Wang Lin. Wang was a kind man, ready to help those in need, but on this occasion, he was really frightened. He dared not express his anger but served them with good food instead.

However, once the bandits came into the house, it was very hard to send them away. With a very sad expression on his face, Wang did not know how to deal with it but gave long sighs.

At that time Wang's sadness aroused attention of his daughter-in-law Chen.

木杆将蜡烛打灭，屋里顿时漆黑一片。陈申如再用腊木杆左右一阵乱打，然后纵身过去，伸手抓住墙上的一个木橛儿，施展轻功将自个儿挂在了墙上。这就是传说中的贴墙挂画神功。

陈恂如将陈申如推进屋后，再把手中的半袋豌豆倒进了屋里地下，响马踩上，站立不稳，纷纷倒地，有往外跑者，被陈恂如一棍一个，打翻捆上。

响马们没有料到会有这样一仗，明知道有人进屋，纷纷操刀，乱砍乱杀，自相残杀，惨叫不绝。

十三个响马悉数被陈恂如捉拿捆住，全部俘获，被县令斩首。平皋村将此事编成一部叫作《双英破敌》的戏曲，传唱乡里一直到现在。

## 七、巧妞失手陈门立规

话说《双英破敌》传唱之后，陈恂如、陈申如名扬怀庆府八县，许多有女之家托人上门提亲，陈所乐推三推四，好容易推到俩儿子十八岁上，同时定婚成亲。

迎娶之后，恂如妻生了一个儿子，申如妻生了一个闺女。陈所乐给孙子起名叫陈嵩，给孙女起名陈巧妞。

巧妞出生一年后，陈申如突然害了一场大病，遍请名医，药石无效，撒手人寰，撇下了妻子高氏与女儿巧妞。高氏暗下决心为夫守节，一心要将女儿抚养成人。

恂如与申如是孪生兄弟，自小亲如一人。失去申如，恂如悲痛欲绝，将自己对弟弟的感情都倾注到侄女巧妞身上。恂如对待侄女巧妞视同己出，从小就带着巧妞与自己的孩子一起习练太极拳。

巧妞虽说是个女孩子，但是父亲陈申如、伯父陈恂如、爷爷陈所乐都是太极拳大师，俗话说得好，"门里出身，自带三分"。更何况巧妞还有伯父恂如的悉心传授，加之自身悟性又高，经过勤学苦练，

She asked her father-in-law, "Is there anything that is troubling you?" "A dozen of bandits are now in our house looking for trouble," Wang said.

Hearing the news, Chen said, "Please prepare a horse for me and I will go to my father's home."

Wang knew that her daughter-in-law's father was very good at Taijiquan and immediately asked a servant to prepare a horse for her. Then Chen went to the Chenjiagou Village in a hurry by riding the horse to ask her father Chen Suole for help.

When he found his daughter arriving on a horse, Chen Suole was very surprised and eagerly asked her what had happened. Hearing her statement of the whole story, Chen Suole laughed and said, "My dear daughter, please go back and tell your father-in-law to prepare food for those bandits, but not serve the meal until it gets dark and candles are lit. Don't worry! Everything will be done well."

When Chen came back to Pinggao Village, she told the entire thing to her father-in-law. After learning that it was Chen Suole's idea, Wang felt greatly relieved and began to make arrangements at once.

When it was nearly dark, Chen Suole asked his twin sons to come to him and said, "After a while you bring weapons and half a bag of peas, and go to your sister's home to deal with a group of bandits."

Hearing the news the brothers were very happy and excited, since they liked this sort of task best. The brothers went to Pinggao Village and ran up to the hall of their sister's home. When they came to the doorway of the hall, they found that the inside of the room was brightly lit and those bandits were enjoying the food and alcohol and shouting loudly.

Holding a stick of Chinese ash in his hand, Chen Shenru asked his brother in a low voice, "Who should enter the room first?" Chen Xunru said, "Don't talk any more," and pushed him into the room.

Rolling into the room, Chen Shenru put out the candle light with a stick, and immediately the room got completely dark. He struck around aimlessly with the stick, and then jumped to hold the wood peg on the wall, hanging himself there by using his brilliant internal power.

After pushing Chen Shenru into the room, Chen Xunru threw the half bag of peas onto the floor of the room. Many of those bandits fell down as soon as they stood on the peas. Some of them ran out of the door, but were struck to the

技艺精进，到十五岁，巧妞已经熟练掌握了曾祖陈王廷所创的太极拳术，在兄妹中独占鳌头。

一家有女百家求。巧妞出落成一个水灵灵、俊生生的大姑娘了，武艺又好，不少的求婚者托人上门，平皋村张家也托人来提亲。

林子大了，什么鸟都有。平皋村里好人多，但也有心怀叵测之徒，张狗剩爷儿俩就是。张狗剩出生时，他父母怕他活不了，就想让儿子在狗嘴里讨个活路，便起名叫狗剩，意思是死了狗也不叼尸体，那就只有活下来了。这张狗剩后来发了不义之财，一夜暴富。因为害怕自己做的坏事暴露，就用脏钱收买了官府中的一些不三不四之人，狐假虎威，专行坑蒙拐骗的勾当。这张狗剩有个独生子叫张孬，比他爹更坏，贪财好色，欺男霸女，无恶不做，为所欲为。

得知巧妞是个才艺双全的好姑娘，张狗剩与张孬爷儿俩起了孬心，张狗剩托人去陈家沟给儿子张孬提亲。

好事不出门，赖事传千里。陈家早知道张狗剩爷儿俩不是东西，就严词拒绝。张狗剩与张孬从此怀恨在心。

常言道，"无巧不成书"。巧妞最后成亲时，还是嫁到了平皋村，女婿与公爹都是本分人。这张孬三天两头上门找事，在巧妞身上动手动脚，百般调戏。因为张家有钱有势，巧妞的公爹和女婿得罪不起，巧妞也只好打掉了牙往肚里咽，忍下这口气。

这一天，巧妞家人都去黄河滩耕地了，巧妞在家做好饭去送，在地头正好碰见了张孬带着家丁在寻事，与公爹和丈夫争吵不停。

张孬一见巧妞来到，立即动了坏心眼，吩咐家丁殴打巧妞的公爹和丈夫，连声吆喝："给我往死里打，打死她家男人，让她当寡妇！"

眼看着公爹和丈夫被毒打得在地上乱滚，性命不保，巧妞怒从心头起，抢起手中送饭挑担的扁担，上前与张孬等人搏斗。

公爹见巧妞出手，也大喊："打死这个王八蛋，大不了爹我去坐牢！"一语成谶。正在张牙舞爪的张孬，被巧妞一扁担打在头顶，栽

ground and bound by Chen Xunru.

Those bandits did not expect such a fight, but they knew that someone had gotten into the room. Therefore, they waved their knives and swords aimlessly only to wound themselves terribly, with the room full of miserable shouts and cries.

All the thirteen bandits were caught and bound by the brothers, and then were sent to the local government for punishment. Later, the story was turned into a drama named *Twin Brothers Capturing Bandits* by the Pinggao villagers, which has been performed on the stage until today.

## VII. Chen Family Setting a Rule after Chen Qiaoniu Killed a Bully

Since the drama *Twin Brothers Capturing Bandits* was passed down among people, Chen Xunru and Chen Shenru became well-known all over the eight counties within Huaiqing Prefecture. Therefore, many people wanted their daughters to get engaged with the brothers, but they were refused politely by Chen Suole. When the brothers grew up to be eighteen years old, they got engaged and were married one after another.

Later, Chen Xunru's wife gave birth to a son named Chen Song, while Chen Shenru's wife to a daughter named Chen Qiaoniu.

At the next year after Chen Qiaoniu was born, Chen Shenru got a serious disease unexpectedly. Many doctors had been invited to treat the disease, but unfortunately he still passed away, leaving his wife Gao and his daughter Chen Qiaoniu. Gao made up her mind not to get remarried but to bring up her daughter with all her heart.

As the twin brother of Chen Shenru, Chen Xunru was extremely saddened by his death, and gave all his love to his niece. He treated her as if she were his daughter and asked her to practice Taijiquan together with his own children.

Since her father Chen Shenru, her uncle Chen Xunru and her grandpa Chen Suole were all Taijiquan masters, Chen Qiaoniu was favorably influenced by the atmosphere of the *wushu* family since childhood. Therefore, she achieved a very good command of Taijiquan created by her grand grandfather Chen Wangting at the age of fifteen because of her diligence and quick-wittedness, and she was

倒在地，气绝身亡。

巧妞的公爹说到做到，真的揽下了所有罪名，蹲了大牢。陈恂如得知事情前后经过，非常痛心地说道："巧妞是个女孩家，拿握不住轻重，害得公爹替罪。以后，陈家拳术传男不传女。"

## 八、陈敬柏神靠除霸

陈敬柏是太极拳的第四代宗师。自幼学习家传太极拳法，拳艺高超，擅长用靠。靠是太极拳独有的打法，主要是利用躯干的力量发力，威力极大，气势恢宏。陈敬柏曾在山东巡抚衙门当差，身经百战，无往不胜，人送雅号"盖山东"。年纪大了，陈敬柏就告老还乡，平时也教些弟子，安享晚年。

有一年夏初的三月二十三，适逢陈家沟村有集会，六十多岁的陈敬柏也到集市上走动，看看热闹。大街上有一处围了一大群人，不时有叫好之声。在一个草帽摊前，陈敬柏买了一顶草帽，戴上遮挡阳光，然后随着人群也向围观处走去。

只见人群当中的空地上，一个肥头大耳、面目狰狞的人正在信口吆喝："人们都说陈家沟卧虎藏龙，高手如云，我看未必见得！今天我王定国在此献艺，如果谁能在我舞刀之时，将一碗水泼在我的头上，我就给他磕三个响头，称他为师！"

说罢，王定国操起一把单刀，缠头裹脑地舞了起来，倏倏倏，刀光闪闪形成光环，罩在王定国头上，真个是风雨不透，围观者不时叫好。

陈敬柏虽说年过花甲，但他见王定国自吹自擂，还贬低陈家沟，心中有些不高兴，就想跟王定国开个玩笑，让他知道知道"天外有天，山外有山"。于是老头凑到王定国身边，伸手取下自己的草帽，瞅准空当，呼地一下给王定国扣在了头上。

better than any of her brothers and sisters.

When Chen Qiaoniu grew up, she was very beautiful and skillful at martial arts, so many people wanted their sons to be engaged with her. One of them was Zhang Gousheng in the Pinggao Village.

People in the Pinggao Village were mostly kind and ready to help others, while Zhang Gousheng and his son were among the few exceptions. The name of "Gousheng" in Chinese originally means that dogs do not touch the body after someone is dead. The reason why his parents gave him this name is that they hoped he could survive in the hard time. Once he got a big fortune by illegal means and became rich overnight. To cover his bad behavior, he took some of the money to bribe some immoral officials and did many bad things. He had a son, his only child, named Zhang Nao, who was even worse. Zhang Nao had a strong lust for money and women, bullied others as he liked, and committed all sorts of wickedness.

Knowing that Chen Qiaoniu was so beautiful and talented, Zhang Gousheng and his son Zhang Nao decided to ask a matchmaker to propose a marriage.

Bad news travels fast. Chen family had already known the evil stories of Zhang Gousheng and his son, so they strongly refused the proposal. From then on, Zhang Gousheng and his son bore a grudge against them.

There is no story without coincidences. Later, Chen Qiaoniu got married with a man from the Pinggao Village. Both her husband and father-in-law were kind and honest, but Zhang Nao often came to make troubles, even molested her in many ways. Since Zhang was rich and powerful, her husband and father-in-law could not afford to offend him, and Chen Qiaoniu had no choice but to bear it in silence.

One day when Chen Qiaoniu's husband and father-in-law were working the land on the Yellow River beach, Zhang Nao and his servants came to make trouble. At that moment, Chen Qiaoniu was just bringing a meal for her family.

Noticing Chen Qiaoniu's coming, Zhang Nao immediately had an evil idea. He asked his servants to give Chen's husband and father-in-law a good beating, and said, "Beat them to death and let her become a widow!"

Seeing that her husband and father-in-law were beaten on the ground so badly that their lives were even endangered, Chen Qiaoniu could not bear any more and waved the pole, which was used to carry the meal, to fight against those bad men.

After the father-in-law found that Chen Qiaoniu had joined the fighting, he

"嗷——好!"见陈敬柏将草帽戴在了王定国头上,围观的人一阵叫好。刚吹过大话的王定国一下子傻了眼,别说一碗水泼头上了,人家把草帽都给自己戴上了,这比当场扇耳光都难受。

"磕头!拜师!""磕头!拜师!"人们开始起哄。

王定国赤红着脸,走到陈敬柏跟前,跪下来,咚咚咚连磕三个响头,问陈敬柏道:"敢问师父大名?"陈敬柏也见得多了,顺口道:"陈家沟人陈敬柏。"王定国记在心头,说:"我王定国今天算是栽在陈家沟了,二十年后一定再来请教!"说罢起身,忿忿而去。

陈敬柏把这事就当一阵风,刮过了什么也就没有了,却不料,二十年之后,王定国还真的来陈家沟寻仇了。

王定国直接找到陈敬柏家,家人不认识王定国,只说是进城去了。

王定国顺着清风岭向县城走,没走多远就看见一位老头骑着毛驴迎面过来,老头正是陈敬柏。王定国上前一把拽住毛驴,向陈敬柏道:"在下王定国前来讨教!"

陈敬柏打死王定国
Chen Jingbai Killing Wang Dingguo in the Fight

cried angrily, "Kill that hooligan and I will go to the prison for you!" No one knew that the saying would unfortunately come true. When Zhang Nao was fighting fiercely, he was struck on the head with the pole by Chen Qiaoniu. As a result, he fell down to the ground at once and was dead.

As he said before, Chen Qiaoniu's father-in-law shouldered the blame for the crime and went to prison. Knowing the whole story, Chen Xunru said very sorrowfully, "As a young woman, Chen Qiaoniu could not carefully control her striking force, resulting in the imprisonment of her father-in-law. From now on, Chen family Taijiquan is allowed to be passed on only among men and boys rather than women and girls."

## Ⅷ. Chen Jingbai Killing a Bully by His Powerful Shouldering

Chen Jingbai, one of the 4th generation masters of Taijiquan, had practiced Taijiquan since childhood and achieved much in martial arts. He was especially good at the technique of Shouldering, one of the peculiar skills of Taijiquan, by which powerful energy could be released from the body. He was even a policeman in Shandong Province, and had experienced lots of fighting without losing. Therefore, he was praised as "Number One in Shandong". When he got into the old age, he returned to his home to enjoy the rest of his life. At the same time, he taught some students Taijiquan.

One day at the beginning of summer, there was a fair in Chenjiagou Village. Chen Jingbai, who was in his sixties then, was touring the fair to kill time. At a corner on the street there was a crowd of people who shouted and cheered occasionally. He bought a straw hat and then went toward that corner.

He found that on the ground surrounded by lots of people, a bad-looking man with a large head and big ears was shouting, "It is said that there are many *wushu* masters in Chengjiagou, but I don't think so. I am Wang Dingguo, and now I am showing my martial arts. If someone is able to pour one bowl of water onto my head while I am waving my knife, I will kowtow to him three times sincerely and call him my master."

Then Wang Dingguo took a knife and waved it above his head quickly as if a powerful shield was formed to prevent anything from entering it. This attracted

八十多岁的陈敬柏早已忘了此人此事，见王定国果真前来，知道是来者不善，就问王定国想怎么办。王定国说你跟我来。他将陈敬柏领到陈家沟玉皇庙内的一间屋子里，进门就搬起一根条石，将玉皇庙大门堵上然后说："咱们今天只能有一个人活着出去！陈敬柏，我已经等你二十年了！"

陈敬柏一听，知道今天不出手是不行了，王定国已起了杀心。于是说："你动手吧！"

王定国也不客气，招招毒手直逼陈敬柏。

陈敬柏让过三招之后，瞅个破绽，贴了上去。陈敬柏一个迎门靠，将王定国腾空击起。王定国从空中跌下来，正好头下脚上撞在自个儿搬来的挡门条石上，顿时脑浆迸溅，一命呜呼！

## 九、太极神肘陈继夏

王定国不服陈家沟卧虎藏龙，命丧八旬老人之手。其实陈家沟太极高手何止一人，太极拳第四代宗师陈继夏不仅武艺超群，而且还是丹青妙手。

陈继夏为人和善，平日里将太极拳的内劲练习融入劳作之中。陈继夏家里以磨面为生，他便借推磨来练习内功。开始之时，陈继夏也是双手推磨，慢慢改用单手推磨，后来用四指、三指，直至最后单指推磨，众人见了无不称奇，陈继夏却不以为然，只道是推磨小技，不足称道。

借推磨练就了太极内功，陈继夏更将太极拳艺练得炉火纯青，尤其以用肘而闻名武林，江湖上便有了"陈敬柏靠，陈继夏肘"的美称。

陈继夏除了习练太极拳之外，还研修山水画法，经常被人请去为厅堂楼阁作壁画，既是创作，又能谋生，陈继夏乐此不疲，怡然

lots of shouts and cheers from the people around him.

Hearing that Wang Dingguo was boasting of his own skills and also belittled masters from Chengjiagou, Chen Jingbai felt a little unhappy. Although he was already over sixty years old, he decided to make fun of him and reminded him that there were mountains beyond the mountains. Then Chen walked to the side of Wang, took off his hat and suddenly put down it right on Wang's head.

"Wonderful," those people around shouted. Wang was greatly stunned and felt very bad. He realized that what he had said just now was purely a bragger's talk. Putting a hat on the head was really much more humiliating than pouring a bowl of water on the head.

"Kowtow and call him master!" "Kowtow and call him master!" People began to shout.

With a blushing face, Wang walked to the front of Chen, knelt down and kowtowed three times with loud noise. Then he asked, "My master, could you tell me your name please?" Chen had experienced such similar occasions many times, so he said without thinking much, "I am Chen Jingbai from Chengjiagou." Wang bore it in his mind and said, "Today I lost the fight in Chenjiagou, but I will return in twenty years!" Then he stood up and left angrily.

Soon Chen Jingbai forgot all this stuff completely, but he had never expected that Wang Dingguo would really return to Chenjiagou to take revenge on him twenty years later.

Wang asked villagers where Chen Jingbai lived and came up to his house. Chen's family did not know Wang, and told him that Chen had gone to the county center.

Then Wang went along the Qingfeng Ridge to the county to look for Chen. Soon, he saw from the distance an old man riding a donkey coming. This man was none other than Chen Jingbai. Wang went up to stop the donkey and said to Chen, "I am Wang Dingguo and want to have a martial art competition with you now."

Chen Jingbai was then over eighty years old and had already forgotten this man and what had happened to them before. Founding that Wang came here as he had promised, Chen realized that he was determined to challenge him. Then he asked Wang about his intention of this travel. Wang asked Chen to follow him into a room in the Yuhuang Temple of Chenjiagou Village, and blocked the door from

自得。

这一天,陈继夏正在一座寺中大殿里作画,急听身后有轻微的脚步声响,他以为是乡亲们来看自己作画,也不在意,只顾自己作画。

突然间,陈继夏感觉脑后一阵疾风袭来,立刻知道有人偷袭。霎那间,对方两只大手已按住了自己的双肩,劲力直透骨肉。陈继夏明白,来人乃武林高手。他暗运内力,一抖双肩,只听见来人一声惊呼,已从陈继夏的头顶飞过,跌落在陈继夏的面前。

偷袭之人也是武林高手,一个空中转体,落在地上,早已震碎了几块铺地的方砖。

你道来人是谁?那也是著名武术家,黄河南岸汜水县人苌乃周,也就是后来苌家拳的创始人。

苌乃周多年习武,潜心研究周易阴阳变化之理,终觉获益不深,素闻陈家沟太极拳博大精深,阴阳互换,刚柔相济,总是没有亲眼目睹。这次渡河而来,就是专门前来拜访太极拳大师陈继夏。此番偷袭,原是为证实人们传说的陈继夏功夫真假。领教之后,急忙施礼拜上,自报家门,请陈继夏原谅自己的鲁莽。

陈继夏对苌乃周也早就有所耳闻,今日一见,分外高兴。从此以后,陈继夏与苌乃周两人成为至交,经常在一起谈文论武,切磋技艺。

话说有一天,陈继夏从苌乃周那里访友交流归来,正遇见两头公牛在街头抵架,斗得那是互不相让,头破血流。一群围观者怕有牛斗败受伤而死,但又无法阻止,急得乱吆喝,可两头公牛已经斗红了眼,丝毫不理。

陈继夏见状,一个箭步跃到街中,伸双手扭住两只牛头上的犄角,将两头牛生生掰开。公牛急得乱踢乱叫,却挣扎不脱。陈继夏双手一抖,将两头牛掀出三四步开外,吓得两头牛顾不上争斗,各自逃窜。众乡亲见陈继夏此举,个个伸出大拇指称赞。

the inside with a stone tablet. Then he said to Chen, "Chen Jingbai, I have waited for twenty years. It's a death fight today, and only one of us can go out of this door!"

Chen Jingbai knew that he had to fight back seriously since Wang was determined to kill him. Then he said to the man, "You start first!"

Wang did not show any politeness and attacked Chen with the intention of killing him.

After three rounds of fighting, Chen took advantage of Wang's weakness and came close to him. By using his powerful Shouldering, he threw Wang up to the air. Falling down from the air, Wang happened to hit the blocking stone head over heels. Immediately Wang was killed, with his head crushed into pieces.

## IX. Chen Jixia, Well-known for His Elbowing

As mentioned in the previous section, Wang Dingguo did not think that there was any *wushu* master in Chenjiagou, but was killed by Chen Jingbai, an eighty-year-old man from the village. Actually, apart from Chen Jingbai, there were many other skillful masters. One of them was Chen Jixia, the fourth generation master, who was good not only at martial arts, but also at Chinese painting.

Chen Jixia was kind to others and liked to practice his internal energy of Taijiquan while doing manual labors. Since he made his living mainly by grinding flour, he often practiced the internal energy through pushing the millstone. At the beginning, he used both hands to push the millstone, gradually by one hand, then by four fingers, by three fingers, and finally by a single finger. It has always been praised as an amazing act while Chen modestly considered it as an unimportant flour-grinding skill.

Apart from the peculiar way of obtaining excellent internal energy, Chen Jixia was also very good at Taijiquan skills, particularly at the elbow skill, which was well-known in the *wushu* circle. Therefore, it was widely accepted that "Chen Jingbai's Shouldering" and "Chen Jixia's Elbowing" were two wonderful fighting skills.

In addition to Taijiquan practice, Chen Jixia also worked hard in drawing landscape paintings, and therefore was often invited to draw wall paintings for others. He enjoyed it very much, since he could create his own works and also earn a living.

One day, when he was drawing paintings in a temple hall, Chen Jixia heard

## 十、陈公兆力斗疯牛

陈公兆是太极拳的第五代宗师,拳艺精湛自不必讲,为人也是乐善好施。遇到灾荒之年,常设粥场施饭,周济贫民。其传承家学,注重养生,至今在陈家沟仍流传着他的养生秘诀:"三十年不停拳,三十年不饱饭,三十年独自乐,三十年独自眠。"他讲述的养生秘密就是要坚持锻炼,不暴饮暴食,要精神乐观,还要注重节欲,到现在还有不少人遵循沿用。由于太极拳有养生益寿的功能,陈家沟的长寿老人较多。清朝乾隆六十年(1795),弘历皇帝已经是85岁的老人了,为了不逾越祖父康熙在位61年的纪录,就决定禅位于太子。嘉庆皇帝为了彰显父亲的文治武功,定于嘉庆元年(1796)的正月初四,在宁寿宫皇极殿为太上皇举办"千叟宴"以示庆贺,要求全国各地推荐年过70岁,身强体壮、德才兼备、子孙满堂的老人前去京城参加宴会。

陈公兆力斗疯牛
Chen Gongzhao Bringing a Mad Bull under Control

light footsteps around. He thought that some villagers had come to see him draw and paint, so he did not care and kept drawing.

Suddenly, Chen Jixia felt a blast of wind blowing toward his head, and immediately he realized that he could be being attacked from the behind. For an instant, he felt on his shoulders a powerful energy. Chen knew that the man was surely good at martial arts. Then he started his internal energy in silence and then suddenly shook his shoulders. It turned out that the man could not help but cry out with astonishment and was thrown over Chen's head, falling down in front of Chen.

The attacker was also a *wushu* master, and he turned his body in the air and fell down to the ground, shattering several ground tiles into pieces.

Who was he? He turned out to be Chang Naizhou, who was born in Sishui County at the south bank of the Yellow River, the creator of the Chang-family boxing.

Although for years Chang Naizhou had insisted on martial arts studies and practice, he was not quite satisfied with his own martial arts level. He had early heard of the good name of Taijiquan in Chenjiagou for its profoundness and peculiarity in the yin-yang theory, so he decided to come across the Yellow River to pay a special visit to Chen Jixia, one of the Taijiquan masters. Therefore through this attack, he wanted to prove whether the saying that Chen Jixia's kung fu was really wonderful was true or not. After knowing Chen's brilliant martial arts, Chang gave a salute hurriedly, introduced himself briefly and asked for Chen's forgiveness for his crudeness.

Chen had also heard about Chang before, and was very happy to see him in person. From then on, they became very good friends to each other, and often discussed and practiced martial arts together.

One day when Chen Jixia was on his way home after visiting his friend Chang Naizhou, he met with two bulls fighting against each other on the street so fiercely that both of their heads were broken and bleeding. The surrounding people worried that one of the bulls might be defeated and killed, so they shouted eagerly to stop the fight but with no effect.

At this moment, Chen Jixia jumped to the front of the bulls very quickly, and forcefully separated the two bulls by taking their horns. The bulls got quite vexed but could not shake off his hands. Then Chen collected his energy suddenly and threw the bulls three or four steps away by using his elbows. The bulls were quite

陈家沟村虽然年过七旬者众多，但入选进京者仅有二人。一位是太极拳第四代传人，85岁的陈善，一位是太极拳第五代传人，88岁的陈毓英。

两位老人奉旨进京参加"千叟宴"，皇上御赐鎏金匾额"龙章宠赐"，同时赏赐有龙头杖、花荷包、黄马褂、鼻烟壶等，荣耀之至。当时的巡抚、知府与县令，为了庆祝陈家沟两位老人赴京参加"千叟宴"的盛事，择吉日来到陈家沟陈氏宗庙挂匾彰旌。

挂匾那天，陈家沟可是比过年还要热闹，村民们舞狮子、斗老虎、踩高跷、划旱船、扭秧歌，鼓乐齐鸣，鞭炮连响。

进入午时，在一干官员的主持下，神圣庄重的挂匾仪式正式开始。陈善与陈毓英两位老人将朝廷赏赐的礼物供奉到宗庙里的祖宗牌位前，以示荣耀。

这可是多少年也没有遇到的大喜事，一直靠耕读传家的陈家沟陈氏家族何时受过皇帝的接见，何时喝过皇上赏赐的御酒，这次两位老人进京替陈家祖宗长了脸，争了光，所有陈氏族人都扬眉吐气，高兴得找不着北了。更有年少轻狂的，不顾一干朝廷命官在场，只顾自己高兴，点燃鞭炮乱扔乱放。

噼里啪啦，鞭炮声此起彼伏，人们都没有料到危机即将到来。突然间，一头疯牛从街道上猛冲过来，直扑围观人群。

原来，是有好事之人将点燃的花炮扔向正在牛棚吃草的老黄牛，老黄牛受到惊吓，挣脱缰绳，疯跑起来，冲上大街，连顶带撞，已经伤了五六个人。

疯牛可不管什么官员、百姓的，一样地冲撞，直奔宗庙大门而去。

现场官员个个目瞪口呆，被这突发事变吓得不知所措，眼看着就要被疯牛掀翻。就在此时，忽听耳旁响起一声苍劲有力的喝声："大家伙儿闪开，让俺来对付它！"

一位年近八旬、须发皆白的老人冲出人群，赤手空拳，直扑疯

frightened, stopped fighting and ran away at once. The people around saw Chen's miraculous act and all praised him by giving him the thumb up.

## X. Chen Gongzhao Fighting against a Bull

As the fifth generation master of Taijiquan, Chen Gongzhao was very good at *wushu*. In addition, he was very kind and generous, and often gave out food to the poor in the years of famine. Besides, he attached great value to health maintenance and created some ideas such as "insisting on Taijiquan practice for 30 years", "keeping a good diet for 30 years", "maintaining a good mood for 30 years" and "sleeping alone without sex for 30 years". His secrets of keeping healthy were just to keep doing physical exercise, to eat and drink moderately, to have an optimistic mind and to abstain from sexual desire. These ideas are even adopted by many people today. Since Taijiquan is very beneficial to keep healthy and prolong life, there have been many people with longevity in Chenjiagou. In early 1796, in order to show the prosperity of the Qing dynasty and advocate the good practice of respecting the old, the imperial court invited people over 70 years old with virtues and talents to attend the "one-thousand-old-men banquet" in the Ningshou Palace of the capital.

Although there were many people who had been over 70 years old in Chenjiagou that year, only two of them were selected to take part in the banquet in the capital city. One was Chen Shan, 85 years old, the fourth generation lineage holder of Taijiquan, and the other was Chen Yuying, 88 years old, the fifth generation lineage holder of Taijiquan.

At the banquet, the two old men were awarded a horizontal board inscribed by the emperor, as well as many other things including a dragon-head stick, a small bag, an imperial yellow jacket and a snuff bottle. In order to celebrate the honorable event, the province governor, the city mayor and the county magistrate at that time paid a special visit to Chenjiagou and held the ceremony of hanging the horizontal board.

During the ceremony, Chenjiagou was really a merry world, in which villagers performed the lion dance, walked on stilts, rowed a land boat and did the yangko dance, with deafening sound of drums and firecrackers in every corner of the village.

牛。这老人,正是陈公兆。

疯牛见有人敢冲向自己,哞哞直叫,更加张狂,将头一低,用犄角直抵陈公兆。

陈公兆看得真切,伸手抓住牛犄角,往前便领,疯牛发现被人牵制,四蹄蹬地,想要往后撤,陈公兆顺势发力一送,疯牛岂知这是太极拳的四两拨千斤,化打结合,牛力虽大,但已失去控制,扑通一声,被撂倒在地,半晌没有起来,被一干人拖了过去。

官府之人惊吓之余,纷纷伸出大拇指:"老人家真乃神人神力啊!"

When the noon time came, the group of officials started the sacred ceremony of hanging the imperial board. Chen Shan and Chen Yuying brought all the gifts given by the emperor in front of the ancestral memorial tablets to remember this great honor.

It was really a great enjoyable occasion for people in Chenjiagou. In the history of Chen family, no one had ever been met with the emperor before, not to mention drinking the alcohol awarded by the emperor. However, the two elders won a great honor for all the people of Chen family. Therefore, many people, particularly youngsters were so excited that they lit firecrackers as they liked.

The sound of firecrackers came from every direction, and no one had expected that something dangerous would happen. All of a sudden, a mad bull dashed onto the street, running toward the crowd.

The truth was that a naughty boy threw a burning firecracker into a cowshed in which a bull was eating, and that the frightened bull freed from its reins forcefully, ran madly in the street and hurt five or six people.

The mad bull cared nothing and ran toward the gate of the Chenjiagou ancestral temple.

All the present officials were greatly stunned and completely felt at a loss. Indeed, it was really such a dangerous occasion that everyone could be thrown to the ground by the bull. At the crucial time, a vigorous shout came, "Go away! I deal with it!"

An old man, who was nearly eighty years old with grey hair and mustache, was seen to dash out from the crowd and run toward the bull without taking any weapon. He was none other than Chen Gongzhao.

The bull found a man running toward it and became more aggressive. It lowered its head and intended to attack Chen Gongzhao with its horns.

When he founded that the bull was about to attack him, he held its horns and pulled it forward. The bull knew that it was controlled by the man, so it drew back forcefully with all the four legs pushing off the ground. At this moment, Chen suddenly used energy to push the bull. Never knowing the powerful skill of Taijiquan, the bull lost its balance and was thrown heavily onto the ground. It could not get up and was dragged away by some people.

Seeing the whole matter, those officials could not help but praise by giving thumbs up, "The elder Chen is really a miraculous man with miraculous energy!"

# 后　　记

太极拳，发源于河南省温县陈家沟。

自明末清初陈家沟人陈王廷创编太极拳以来，三百多年世代传承，历久不衰，并逐渐衍变出杨氏、武氏、和氏、吴氏、孙氏、李氏、忽雷、腾挪、忽灵、王其和式等多家太极拳流派。

太极拳是辩证的理论思维与武术、艺术、导引术、中医等的完美结合，它以中国传统儒、道学说中的太极、阴阳辩证理念为核心思想，集颐养性情、强身健体、技击对抗等多种功能为一体，是高层次的人体文化。

中国河南省温县陈家沟太极拳国际交流中心
The International Exchange Center for Taijiquan in Chenjiagou, Wenxian, Henan Province of China

太极拳是综合了历代各家拳法，结合易学的阴阳五行之变化、中医经络学、古代的导引术和吐纳术形成的一种内外兼修、柔和、缓慢、轻灵、刚柔相济的拳术，有助于习练者在增强体质的同时提高自身素养，

# Postscript

Taijiquan originated from Chenjiagou, Wenxian County, Henan Province.

Chen Wangting, born in Chenjiagou, created Taijiquan during the end of the Ming and early Qing dynasties. For more than three hundred years of development, Taijiquan gradually evolved into a number of Taijiquan styles, such as Yang style, Wu style, He style, Woo style, Sun style, Li style, Hulei style, Tengnuo style, Huling style and Wang Qihe style.

Taijiquan is a perfect combination of dialectical theoretical thinking and *wushu*, arts, *daoyin* and traditional Chinese medicine. It takes the dialectical idea of yin and yang in traditional Chinese Confucianism and Daoism as the core idea, and integrates various functions such as maintaining temperament, strengthening body, fighting and confrontation, which is a high-level human culture.

Taijiquan is a kind of boxing that combines various martial arts, yin and yang, the Five Elements, the traditional Chinese medicine meridian, and the ancient techniques of *daoyin* and breathing, hence such characteristics as combination of the inner and outer cultivation, gentleness, slowness, agility, and balance between hardness and softness. It also helps its practitioners to improve their literacy, enhance their physique and promote the harmony between man and nature, and between man and society.

It is the features of implicitness and restraint, continuity, overcoming hardness with softness, alternation of quickness and slowness, and naturalness and smoothness that help the practitioners use the mind to control the body. After constant practicing by using mind to guide *qi*, one can attain the supreme realm in mind, *qi*, form and spirit, achieving the goal of cultivating one's morality and strengthening one's body.

As a form of exercise that embraces the concept of oriental inclusiveness, the practitioners are very responsive to the physiological and psychological requirements of human beings for the exercise of mind, *qi*, form and spirit. They are extremely important for the physical and mental health of human beings and the harmonious coexistence of human groups.

Taijiquan, the gem of Chinese martial arts, has been widely praised by people

同时促进人与自然、人与社会的融洽与和谐。

基于太极阴阳之理念，太极拳含蓄内敛、连绵不断、以柔克刚、急缓相间、行云流水的拳术风格，使习练者用意念统领全身，通过入静放松、以意导气、以气催形的反复习练，进入意、气、形、神逐渐趋于圆融一体的至高境界，达到修身养性、陶冶情操、强身健体的目的。

作为一种饱含东方包容理念的运动形式，太极拳习练者针对意、气、形、神的锻炼，非常符合人体生理和心理的需求，对人类个体身心健康以及人类群体的和谐共处，有着极为重要的促进作用。

太极拳作为中华武术瑰宝已受到了世界各地人们的普遍推崇。20世纪80年代以来，中国各级政府及广大民众对太极拳这一古老文化体系的保护意识日益强化，各级政府相继制定保护措施，传承人、民间传承组织也加大深入推广的力度。2006年5月，太极拳被中国政府公布为第一批国家级非物质文化遗产。

为使太极拳这一宝贵的非物质文化遗产项目得到全世界人民更好的保护和利用，中华人民共和国文化和旅游部从2008年起，就开始积极推荐太极拳申报联合国教科文卫组织人类非物质文化遗产代表作。

all over the world. Since the 1980s, the Chinese government and the general public have increasingly strengthened their awareness of protecting the ancient cultural system of Taijiquan. The governments at all levels have successively formulated protective measures, while holders and related organizations have also intensified their efforts to promote the art. In May 2006, Taijiquan was listed by the Chinese government as one of the first batch of items of national intangible cultural heritage.

In order to make Taijiquan get better protected and utilized by people all over the world, the Ministry of Culture and Tourism of the People's Republic of China has been actively recommending Taijiquan to be declared as a masterpiece of intangible cultural heritage of humanity by the United Nations Educational, Scientific and Cultural Organization since 2008.

附录一
Appendix I

# 中国历史年代简表
# A Brief Chronology of Chinese History

| | | |
|---|---|---|
| 五帝时代<br>Period of the Five Legendary Rulers<br>c. 2600 BC-c. 2070 BC | 黄帝 Huangdi (Yellow Emperor) | |
| | 颛顼 Zhuanxu | |
| | 帝喾 Diku (Emperor Ku) | |
| | （唐）尧 Yao | |
| | （虞）舜 Shun | |
| 夏 Xia Dynasty | c. 2070 BC— c. 1600 BC | |
| 商 Shang Dynasty | c. 1600 BC— c. 1046 BC | |
| 西周 Western Zhou Dynasty | c. 1046 BC— c. 771 BC | |
| 东周 Eastern Zhou Dynasty 770 BC-256 BC | 春秋 Spring and Autumn Period | 770 BC—476BC |
| | 战国 Warring States Period | 475 BC—221 BC |
| 秦 Qin Dynasty | 221 BC—206 BC | |
| 汉 Han Dynasty 206 BC-220 AD | 西汉 Western Han | 206 BC—25 AD |
| | 东汉 Eastern Han | 25—220 |
| 三国 Three Kingdoms 220-280 | 魏 Wei | 220—265 |
| | 蜀汉 Shu Han | 221—263 |
| | 吴 Wu | 222—280 |
| 晋 Jin Dynasty 265-420 | 西晋 Western Jin | 265—317 |
| | 东晋 Eastern Jin | 317—420 |

续表 Continued Table

| | | | |
|---|---|---|---|
| 南北朝<br>Southern and Northern Dynasties 420—589 | 南朝<br>Southern Dynasties | 宋 Song | 420—479 |
| | | 齐 Qi | 479—502 |
| | | 梁 Liang | 502—557 |
| | | 陈 Chen | 557—589 |
| | 北朝<br>Northern Dynasties | 北魏 Northern Wei | 386—534 |
| | | 东魏 Eastern Wei | 534—550 |
| | | 北齐 Northern Qi | 550—577 |
| | | 西魏 Western Wei | 535—556 |
| | | 北周 Northern Zhou | 557—581 |
| 隋 Sui Dynasty | | | 581-618 |
| 唐 Tang Dynasty | | | 618-907 |
| 五代十国<br>Five Dynasties and Ten States | 五代<br>Five Dynasties<br>907-960 | 后梁 Later Liang | 907—923 |
| | | 后唐 Later Tang | 923—936 |
| | | 后晋 Later Jin | 936—947 |
| | | 后汉 Later Han | 947—950 |
| | | 后周 Later Zhou | 951—960 |
| | 十国<br>Ten States<br>902-979 | 北汉 Northern Han | 951—979 |
| | | 吴 Wu | 902—937 |
| | | 吴越 Wuyue | 907—978 |
| | | 闽 Min | 909—945 |
| | | 南汉 Southern Han | 917—971 |
| | | 荆南(又称"南平")Jingnan (Nanping) | 924—963 |
| | | 楚 Chu | 927—951 |
| | | 南唐 Southern Tang | 937—975 |
| | | 前蜀 Former Shu | 907—925 |
| | | 后蜀 Later Shu | 934—965 |

续表 Continued Table

| 宋<br>Song Dynasty 960-1279 | 北宋<br>Northern Song | 960—1127 |
| --- | --- | --- |
| | 南宋<br>Southern Song | 1127—1279 |
| 辽 Liao ( 契丹 Qidan/Khitan) | 907—1125 | |
| 金 Jin | 1115—1234 | |
| 西夏 Xixia (Tangut) | 1038—1227 | |
| 元 Yuan Dynasty | 1206—1368 | |
| 明 Ming Dynasty | 1368—1644 | |
| 清 Qing Dynasty | 1616—1911 | |
| 中华民国<br>Republic of China | 1912—1949 | |
| 中华人民共和国<br>People's Republic of China | 1949— | |

# 附录二
# Appendix Ⅱ

## 专用词表（汉英）
## Glossary (Chinese-English)

| 基本概念 | **Basic Concepts** |
|---|---|
| 太极拳 | Taijiquan |
| 陈式太极拳 | Chen style Taijiquan |
| 陈家沟 | Chenjiagou |
| 推手 | pushing hands |
| 套路 | routine |
| 意 | intention |
| 气 | *qi* |
| 形 | form |
| 神 | spirit |
| 心 | mind |
| 劲 | *jin* |
| 力 | force |
| 虚 | emptiness |
| 实 | fullness |

| 太极拳技 | **Techniques of Taijiquan** |
|---|---|
| 太极拳大架 | the Big Frame of Taijiquan |
| 太极拳小架 | the Small Frame of Taijiquan |
| 缠丝劲 | the silk-reeling *jin* |

| | |
|---|---|
| 十三势 | thirteen postures |
| 五步 | five footwork methods |
| 八法 | eight techniques |
| 掤 | Warding off |
| 捋 | Rolling back |
| 挤 | Pressing |
| 按 | Pushing |
| 採 | Pulling down |
| 挒 | Splitting |
| 肘 | Elbowing |
| 靠 | Shouldering |
| 粘 | Adhering |
| 连 | Connecting |
| 黏 | Sticking |
| 随 | Following |

## 太极拳理 — Theory of Taijiquan

| | |
|---|---|
| 天人合一 | harmony between man and nature |
| 以柔克刚 | to overcome hardness with softness |
| 以意领行 | to guide moves by intention |
| 沉肩坠肘 | to lower the shoulders and elbows |
| 懂劲 | to comprehend *jin* |
| 刚柔相济 | to keep the balance between hardness and softness |
| 含胸拔背 | to contract the chest and broaden the back |
| 节节贯串 | to coordinate every part of the body |
| 快慢相间 | to alternate quickness with slowness |

| | |
|---|---|
| 气沉丹田 | to sink *qi* to dantian |
| 松腰圆裆 | to relax the waist and arch the crotch |
| 虚领顶劲 | to keep the head upright naturally |
| 不丢不顶 | neither releasing nor resisting |

**经典著述**      **Classics**

| | |
|---|---|
| 《陈氏太极拳图说》 | *The Illustrated Canon of Chen Style Taijiquan* |
| 《太极拳术》 | *The Art of Taijiquan* |
| 《太极拳体用全书》 | *Essence and Applications of Taijiquan* |
| 《五字诀》 | *Song of Five Characters* |
| 《撒放秘诀》 | *Secrets on Releasing* |
| 《太极拳小序》 | *Short Preface of Taijiquan* |
| 《走架打手行功要言》 | *Essentials of Fighting* |
| 《黄庭经》 | *Huang Ting Jing* (*The Yellow Court Classic*) |